AM I
Being Deceived?

AM I
Being Deceived?

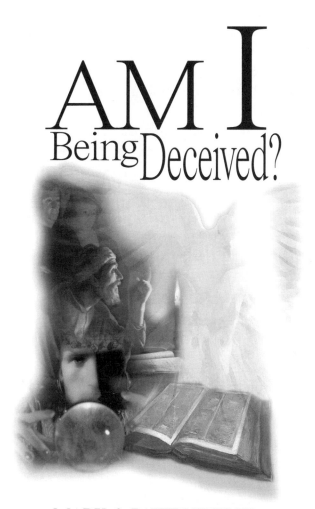

MARK & PATTI VIRKLER

Bridge-Logos *Publishers*

Gainesville, Florida 32614 USA

Unless otherwise indicated, the Scripture quotations in this publication are from the King James Version of the Bible.

Am I Being Deceived?
by Mark and Patti Virkler

Copyright © 2001 by Mark and Patti Virkler
Library of Congress Catalog Card Number: Pending
International Standard Book Number: 0-88270-866-X

Published by:
Bridge-Logos *Publishers*
PO Box 141630
Gainesville, FL 32614
http://www.bridgelogos.com

TABLE OF CONTENTS

SO WHY WAS THIS BOOK WRITTEN?

This book is written for the Christian who is pressing on in the ways of the Holy Spirit. It will help clarify some of the boundaries, things to avoid, and what should be pressed toward. It will also help define Phariseeism. When attacked by Pharisees for pressing into the ways of the Holy Spirit, readers will be more readily able to understand their beliefs as well as the mindset of the attacker. They will be able to respond with biblical conviction knowing full well that they are neither New Age nor Pharisee but Christian. Even though there may be incessant attacks by Pharisees for being a member of the New Age movement, this book will equip with biblical and theological structures offering comfort and strengthening hearts.

FOREWORD

Mark and Patti Virkler have performed a great service to the Body of Christ with this book. It is both grievous and amazing that Christians have been so seemingly paranoid regarding issues associated with the New Age movement. While the Bible does indeed call us to be wise as serpents and not allow our thinking to go astray, it also tells us that greater is He that is in us than he that is in the world. Could it be that far too many Christians appear to have more faith in the ability of the enemy to pull them off course than they do in God to keep them secure?

It is this "paranoia" that has made many of the insights God has given the Virklers so controversial over the years. From their life-changing teachings, I have seen and heard a range of reactions. Two are, "among the most spiritually significant experiences of my life," and "we cannot have this kind of teaching in our midst." Believe it or not, both of these comments came from members of the same congregation.

It was a discussion of the mixed reaction to the Virkler's teachings that inspired this book. Exasperated with the fearful reaction of some, I proposed to Mark that we desperately needed a book to help Christians see the New Age movement for what it really is. Satan successfully robs many in the Church from a great deal of helpful wisdom through the shopworn guilt by association ploy.

Because of some unique health challenges, my wife and I choose to eat "healthy." Because this is not mainstream thinking (just check out any grocery store), we frequently find ourselves in health food stores purchasing groceries alongside customers purchasing crystals, weird books, and healthy food. Often we are criticized by well meaning Christians for even entering such a store, let alone supporting its proprietor with our Christian money. But as John 17 so clearly teaches, we're sent to the world. Most Christians lack the understanding that the United States is now the third largest mission field in the world, measured by the number of unbelievers in the population (exceeded only by India and China). As Leonard Sweet writes in *SoulTsunami*, "Postmodern evangelism doesn't say to the world, 'Come to church.' Rather, it says to the Church, 'Go to the world.'" He goes on to write that we must not retreat from the church or withdraw from the world, but stay where we are and resist the pagan ways of living.

I have read a great deal of what I term "success" literature; books that are designed to help people succeed in life, according to their definition of success. I find it quite interesting that almost all the principles taught in these success books are found in Scripture. That being the case, one would expect Christians to be among the most successful people in the world. And while in a spiritual sense, they indeed may be, certainly in a physical sense Christians seem to be as mediocre, if not more so, than the rest of the world. In fact, in some Christian circles, physical and fiscal successes are signals for great suspicion. The greatest overcomers in the world are all too often not Christians. It's the non-Christians who are doing a better job of living by biblical principles learned from being open-minded to pragmatic teaching. Once again, even though the principles are in the Bible, the enemy has created an environment where many Christians run from those principles simply because they feel guilty of being used by the world.

These fearful ideas simply should not be. We, as disciples of Christ, need to learn to rest secure in the arms of our Lord, believing that He will protect us from the guiles of the enemy. We need to become so familiar with the real that as soon as we encounter the deceitful, red flags will go up instantly. This idea seems difficult for the Virklers' students to understand. We need to be able to "eat the meat and spit out the bones." There is much wisdom (and common sense) that the enemy has succeeded in robbing us of because of our overly suspicious minds.

I am excited to recommend *Are You Being Deceived?*. It contrasts the beauty of the real with the sometimes not so subtle ugliness of the deceitful. It not only looks at New Age thinking, but also looks at the deception inherent in those caught up in the opposite extreme, legalism or Pharaseeism. Satan is indeed a wry old buzzard, prowling around looking for victims to devour. I pray the Church will devour this book and that the truth will emerge, allowing Christians to be better equipped as salt and light to the world.

Jerry Graham

INTRODUCTION

THE REAL AND
TWO DEMONIC COUNTERFEITS

To detect counterfeits, one must first be taught to recognize the real. He must examine it inside and out so he knows its chief distinguishing features. The counterfeits will miss some of these features and thus be found out. This is how bank tellers are trained to recognize counterfeit bills: they get to know the true bill. So we will begin by examining the real which is Christianity. Then, we will look at two counterfeits, the New Age Movement and Phariseeism. Contrasts and comparisons will be included.

As we make these comparisons you will discover that of the two counterfeits, New Age is much closer to true Christianity than Phariseeism. Of course, neither counterfeit is right. Christianity is right, and both counterfeits are wrong.

Obviously, although some may stand up and declare proudly that they are "New Agers," no one stands up and declares that he is a Pharisee. There are probably several reasons for that. One is that most people in the Church have not examined the traits of Phariseeism, so they are not even aware on a conscious level of exactly what Phariseeism is. Secondly, if one did discover that he were indeed a Pharisee, he probably would not want to declare that fact publicly. If he were truly seeking God, he would repent of his Phariseeism and get over it. If he were just religious, and not really ready to lay his life down for God, then he would most likely become stiff-necked, resisting the identification with his father the devil, and would do everything in his power to kill the messenger of God who caused him to see that (Acts 7:51,52).

A true Pharisee questions authority (Matt. 21:23), seeks to kill and destroy (Matt. 12:14), and has a heathen heart (Acts 7:51). He is blind (Jn 12:37-40); judgmental (Matt. 7:1-6); easily offended (Matt. 13:53-58); disobedient (Matt. 23:2,3); condemnatory (Matt. 9:3); accusatory (Jn. 8:48; 10:20); proud, and deaf to the truth (Acts 7:51). And he is not inclined to repent when confronted with his sin.

According to Scripture, Pharisees carry the spirit of murder with them (Jn. 8:44). I have no desire to be murdered. So it seems wisest to simply present the truth to those who are seeking truth, without endangering my life by exposing my identity to those who killed the Son of God. I debated long and hard about whether I would list my name as the author; however, in final analysis, I have gone ahead and done so. I hope it is a wise decision. I am not interested in being murdered, so if you are a committed Pharisee then I would ask that you not take the time to read this book.

Satan's favorite tactic when he is designing what he considers a good counterfeit is to mix some truth in with some error. If there isn't at least an element of truth, few will receive it. So satan mixes in truth to see if he can deceive many with a counterfeit.

One Extreme Is the Bible Without the Spirit - Phariseeism

As was the case in Jesus' day, Pharisees are Bible-thumpers. They are big on the Bible. They study it, memorize it, interpret it, and apply it to their lives as best they know how.

However, their traditions invalidate the Word of God, and negate the power of God in their midst (Mk. 7:13). Because they are not open to the Spirit or revelation knowledge, they come against those who walk in the Spirit, persecuting and seeking to murder them (Acts 7; Gal. 3, 4). Paul is a perfect example of a Pharisee who was murdering Christians until God gave him a revelatory experience on the road to Damascus where he heard God's voice and saw a vision. From that point on his life was reversed - he came alongside the Spirit-filled Christians whom he had been trying to kill, and he came against the Pharisees, of whom he had been a chief.

Because Pharisees aren't open to the Holy Spirit, they didn't show up at the birth of Jesus. Shepherds who could see visions of angels singing recognized Jesus' birth (Lk. 2:8-16). Wise men who could discern the message of God in His creation (the stars) showed up (Matt. 2:1,2). Simeon, a righteous and devout man who had the Holy Spirit upon him, was led by the Spirit to the temple to prophesy over Jesus (Lk. 2:25-32). But no Bible-thumper recognized Jesus' birth; only those who were open to revelation knowledge and spiritual experiences.

In this way, Pharisees miss the moving of God in their own generation. They are fixed on the laws of God from generations ago, and are adamantly opposed to any direct encounter with God themselves. They have built a religious set of rules and principles telling about a God Who lived and moved and acted miraculously in days past. However, there is no direct interaction with Him today in their lives.

Obviously, this is not Christianity, because Christianity demands a direct encounter and a personal relationship with God through His Son Jesus Christ. When I was a Pharisee myself, I actually held a theology declaring that I had a personal relationship with God and with Jesus. I had invited Jesus Christ into my heart as my Lord and Savior. However, I was instructed that I was not to expect any feelings, because feelings were soulish. I was not to expect His voice, because I now had the Bible. I was not to expect His vision, because there are no more dreams and visions today. Nor was I to expect His anointing with power, because the age of miracles had passed.

So I ask you, did I have a personal relationship with Jesus, or did I simply have a theology which said that I had a relationship with Jesus? What kind of a relationship is it when you can't hear the person, see the person, feel the person, or sense the person? If you want a relationship like that, you can have it! Personally, I have concluded that it is most likely not a relationship at all. They are just words, saying there is a relationship.

The proof that the Pharisees really didn't have a personal relationship with God, or sense God's Spirit, was that their hearts were filled with murder.

> *For you are the children of your father the Devil, and you love to do the evil things he does. He was a murderer from the beginning and has always hated the truth. There is no truth in him. When he lies, it is consistent with his character for he is a liar and the father of lies (Jn. 8:44 NLT).*

Bible-thumping Pharisees aren't just wrong. Jesus said they are demonic. They are of satan. They are sons of the devil! They are killers. There is no truth in them, even though they spend their lives studying the Bible! Amazing! This is heavy. Most of us would prefer to say, "Well, they might be overly rationalistic, but, thank God, they are not into the New Age cult." Well, you tell me, is having the devil as your father any better than being a New Ager? I seriously doubt it.

So, being a Bible-thumping, anti-Spirit Pharisee is not good, it is not neutral, and it is not better than being a New Ager. If you are a Pharisee, then Jesus says you are not a Christian, even though you may read and study your Bible until you are blue in the face.

The questions, as far as Jesus and the Bible are concerned, are, "Do you accept the Holy Spirit as an integral part of your life, more than just giving Him lip service ?(Jn.14:16,17). Do you live in the Spirit and walk in the Spirit (Gal. 5:25)? Do you hear His voice (Jn. 10:27)? Do you receive His dreams (Acts 2:17)? Do you see His visions (Acts 2:17)? Do you prophesy (Acts 2:17)? Do you operate in the power of God, (i.e., the gifts of the Holy Spirit - I Cor. 12:1-11)? Or is your religion a theology about a God Who used to do these things?" If it is, then the Bible says you are a Pharisee and you need to repent, for you are of your father, the devil. Like Paul, a day came in my life when I discovered that I was a Pharisee, and I repented.

If as you go through this book you do discern, as I did, that you are a pharisee, then I pray that you, too, would choose the path of repentance. I am not here to judge or condemn any man. Before his Maker he stands or falls. I am here to love, pray and intercede for mankind. As Paul, I, too, am a chief of sinners. May your heart be open to the Spirit of God.

As a final note: These Pharisees in their deception will come against true Christians who do believe that the Bible and the Holy Spirit should go hand in hand. Because these true Christians have embraced the Holy Spirit as being alive and active today, Pharisees seek to brand them as New Age. Look how the Pharisees of Jesus' day rejected Him!

> *You rejected this holy, righteous one and instead demanded the release of a murderer (Acts 3:14 NLT).*

How's that for getting everything backward?

Another Extreme Is the Spirit Without the Bible - The New Age

The other cult we will examine in this book is the New Age movement. The New Age movement is at the opposite extreme of Phariseeism, for while Pharisees embrace the Bible and reject the Spirit, New Age embraces the spirit world, but rejects the Bible as being the inerrant Word of God.

So New Agers are out there exploring the world of the spirit without the Bible to act as a compass and help them see what is right and what is wrong. They, too, are headed for destruction unless they embrace the Bible as God's declaration of truth.

New Agers want more than the false idol of rationalism offered by the western world. They realize that life is much larger than that. They realize that there is a spirit world and they are hungry to explore it with every fiber of strength within them. So they will study ESP, try various meditation practices and seek out spiritual modalities for healing and for receiving knowledge. Many of them will make considerable progress in exploring the spiritual world.

Their problem is that they go in unprotected. They are seeking to connect with spiritual powers without discerning that there are both good and evil spiritual powers: God and satan, heaven and hell, right and wrong. They discover some of God and some of satan, and they have no good way to discern which is which, because they have discarded the Bible as an authoritative standard for discovering truth. Without an absolute truth, all "truth" becomes relative, and they enter into a quagmire of error and deception.

New Age followers, too, need to repent and return to the God of Abraham, Isaac, and Jacob. They need to recognize that Jesus Christ is Lord, that He is the Son of God Who died on a cross, and Whose shed blood offers them cleansing for their sins if they will but repent and receive Him as their Lord and Savior. They must also receive the Bible as the inspired Word of God.

It seems to me that the central issue is, "Who is Lord?" The Pharisee says his mind is ruler and in control. Therefore, whatever his mind interprets as being true from the Bible is accepted as truth. A New Ager says whatever his experience in the spirit world dictates to be true is true and is G/god.

The Christian rejects both of these false gods.

Christianity - Where the Bible and the Spirit Meet

The Christian believes that:

The Bible Is Important

All scripture is given by inspiration of God, and is profitable for doctrine, for reproof, for correction, for instruction in righteousness (II Tim. 3:16).

The Spirit Is Important

"And it shall come to pass in the last days," saith God, "I will pour out of my Spirit upon all flesh: and your sons and your daughters shall prophesy, and your young men shall see visions, and your old men shall dream dreams" (Acts 2:17).

The Bible is the historical record of people who had spiritual experiences with Almighty God. This historical record is to be our sounding board when we, too, have experiences with Almighty God.

We have dreams and compare them with biblical dreams. We see visions and we compare them with biblical visions. We hear God's voice and compare it with biblical examples of others who heard God's voice. We prophesy and compare it with others in the Bible who prophesied. We lay hands on the sick and they recover, and we compare our experiences with others in the Bible who laid hands on the sick.

So the Bible is not to replace our personal encounters with God through the Spirit. Rather, it is to serve as a sounding board for us, so that as we have similar spiritual experiences, we can compare them with those who have walked with God before us.

And when it comes to interpreting the Bible, the Christian does not turn to the false god of rationalism who says we are to use our minds and reason about God. No, the Bible never encourages us to reason on our own, but only to reason together with God, allowing our reasoning capacities to be moved upon by the Holy Spirit so that we have anointed reasoning (Is. 1:18).

An example of the Holy Spirit illuminating one's reasoning or understanding can be found in Luke 24:32.

> *And they said one to another, "Did not our heart burn within us, while He talked with us by the way, and while He opened to us the scriptures?"*

When Jesus explains Scripture to us it results in revelation in our hearts which can be experienced as a burning sensation (Lk. 24:27). This is surely much different than the pure analysis of rationalism.

David and Paul both prayed for and hungered for this spiritual revelation as they meditated on the Bible. Paul especially knew that without it, he would be nothing but a Pharisee. Note their prayers.

> *Open thou mine eyes, that I may behold wondrous things out of thy law (Ps. 119:18).*

That the God of our Lord Jesus Christ, the Father of glory, may give unto you the spirit of wisdom and revelation in the knowledge of him: The eyes of your understanding being enlightened; that ye may know what is the hope of his calling, and what the riches of the glory of his inheritance in the saints (Eph. 1:17,18).

A Pharisee would not pray this prayer, because there is no expectation of any direct interaction between the Pharisee and the Holy Spirit when the Bible is studied. A New Ager wouldn't pray this prayer because there is no belief that the Bible is the inspired Word of God, so it probably wouldn't be read with any intensely. However, the Christian will find this prayer on the lips every time the Bible is read, because the Christian knows that if the Holy Spirit doesn't make the Word come alive, it will just be religious principles and not true Christianity.

Our Plan of Attack

As we continue, we will first look at true Christianity, where the Bible and the Spirit flow together. We will then examine the New Age movement where spirit reigns and the Bible is discarded, and finally we will examine Phariseeism where the Bible reigns and the Spirit is discarded.

The Real CHRISTIANITY: *The Bible and the Spirit*

1st Counterfeit NEW AGE MOVEMENT: *The spirit without the Bible*

2nd Counterfeit PHARISEEISM: *The Bible without the Spirit*

1

CHRISTIANITY:
THE BIBLE AND THE SPIRIT

Christianity embraces both the Bible and the Holy Spirit. Let's observe this through the New Testament.

The Christian has a humble heart seeking after God

Blessed are the humble (Matt. 5:3); the repentant (Matt. 5:4); the gentle (Matt. 5:5); those who hunger and thirst for righteousness (Matt. 5:6); the merciful (Matt. 5:7); the pure in heart (Matt. 5:8); the peacemakers (Matt. 5:9); and those who have been persecuted for the sake of righteousness (Matt. 5:10).

The Christian must humble himself as a child in order to enter the kingdom of heaven (Matt. 18:3).

The Christian abides in the written and spoken words of Jesus

Abide in the words (*logos* - written word) of Jesus (Jn. 8:31).

Abide in Jesus and let His words (*rhema* - spoken words) abide in you. Then you can ask whatever you wish, and it shall be done for you. This glorifies the Father and proves that you are His disciples (Jn. 15:7,8).

The Christian has faith that prayer connects him with the ever-present power of God and God's provision for his life

Believes that God is active in his life. He believes that he can ask and receive (Matt. 7:7,8).

Knows he may ask and he will receive, that his joy may be made full (Jn. 16:24).

Understands that two Christians may join together in the name of Jesus and agree on earth about anything that they may ask and it shall be done for them by the Father Who is in heaven (Matt. 18:18-20).

Maintains that if you have faith and do not doubt, you may say to this mountain, be taken up and cast into the sea, and it shall happen. And all things asked in prayer, believing, shall be received (Matt. 21:21,22).

The Christian maintains love for others

He abides in God's love and loves others (Jn. 15:10,12).

He handles his disputes first in private discussions between the offended parties, secondly with two or three witnesses, and finally, if not resolved, by bringing it before the church at large (Matt. 18:15-18).

He forgives his brothers from his heart (Matt. 19:35).

The Christian steers clear of the teaching of legalists and Pharisees

He is aware of the teachings of Pharisees (Matt. 16:6,12).

The Christian lives out of divine initiative by being sensitive to the flow of the Holy Spirit within him which grants God's voice and God's vision

When the Pharisees were trying to kill Jesus for breaking the Sabbath (Jn. 5:18), Jesus made it clear that He was living out of the leading of the Holy Spirit who was showing Him and telling Him what the Father was doing (Jn. 5:19,20,30; 8:26,28,38). His Spirit-led actions were putting

Him at direct odds with the Pharisees. Jesus said that those who hear His voice will live (Jn. 5:25) and that the Pharisees were willing to search the Scriptures for eternal life, but were unwilling to actually come to Jesus so that they would have life (Jn. 5:39,40). They were going to stop short of an actual relationship with Jesus, and simply live out of the Scriptures, not receiving Jesus' life.

The Christian lives out of the Spirit which flows from his innermost being as a river of living water (Jn. 7:37-39).

Note, for example:

An angel of the Lord spoke to Philip saying, "Arise and go..." (Acts 8:26).

And the Spirit said to Philip, "Go up and join this chariot." (Acts 8:29).

The Spirit of the Lord snatched Philip away...But Philip found himself at Azotus... (Acts 8:39,40).

Paul's conversion was instigated by a bright light from heaven flashing around him and a voice speaking to him (Acts 9:3-6). This was followed by Ananias' receiving direction in a vision to go and lay hands on Paul for him to receive his sight. Ananias did, and Paul's sight returned (Acts 9:10-19).

Paul was directed by the Spirit as to where to go (Acts 16:6,7).

Paul was guided by a dream at night (Acts 16:9,10).

The Lord spoke encouragement to Paul in a night vision (Acts 18:9,10).

God encouraged Paul at night with a spoken message (Acts 23:11; 27:23,24).

The Christian relies upon the Holy Spirit when interpreting the Bible, preaching, and receiving revelation

The Pharisees wanted to know how Jesus could speak so powerfully, having never been educated (Jn. 7:15). Jesus' response was, "My teaching is not Mine, but His Who sent me. And those who will do the will of God will know [i.e., have an inner witness in their spirits] whether the teaching is of God or not" (Jn. 7:16,17). Thus, the ability to discern truth and error is only available to those who are living right with God.

The first rule of biblical interpretation: The Holy Spirit bears witness within when you hear the truth - The Holy Spirit, the Spirit of Truth, Who proceeds from the Father, will cause a witness within your heart when you hear truth (Jn. 15:26,27)

The second rule of biblical interpretation: The Holy Spirit guides you into truth - The Holy Spirit, the Spirit of Truth, guides you into all the truth, disclosing things of the Father to you (Jn. 16:13-15).

If you have and keep God's commandments, you love God, and are loved by God, and God will abide with you and disclose Himself to you through the working of the Holy Spirit, Who will teach you all things (Jn. 14:21,23,26).

The third rule of biblical interpretation: You will only see what you can handle - God will only reveal to you what you are able to bear. There is more to say to you, but He will wait until you can bear it (Jn. 16:12).

The fourth rule of biblical interpretation: You cannot interpret the Bible on your own - Know that apart from Jesus you can do nothing, which includes interpret the Bible correctly (Jn. 15:5).

The fifth rule of biblical interpretation: Pray for God to open your heart - Pray that God opens your heart to respond to Him, and the hearts of those to whom you preach to respond to your preaching (Acts 16:14).

The Christian believes in and manifests a supernatural ministry

The Christian is commissioned to heal the sick, raise the dead, cleanse the lepers, cast out demons and to give freely (Matt. 10:8).

Jesus spoke words that are spirit and life; the flesh profits nothing (Jn. 6:63).

The Great Commission:

"All authority has been given to Me in heaven and on earth. Go therefore and make disciples of all the nations, baptizing them in the name of the Father and the Son and the Holy Spirit, teaching them to observe all that I commanded you; and lo, I am with you always, even to the end of the age" (Matt. 28:18-20).

"Go into all the world and preach the gospel to all creation. These signs will accompany those who have believed: in My name they will cast out demons, and they will speak with new tongues; they will pick up serpents, and if they drink any deadly poison, it shall not hurt them; they will lay hands on the sick, and they will recover" (Mk. 16:15-18).

"You shall receive power when the Holy Spirit has come upon you; and you shall be My witnesses both in Jerusalem, and in all Judea and Samaria, and even to the remotest part of the earth" (Acts 1:8).

And they were all filled with the Holy Spirit and began to speak with other tongues, as the Spirit was giving them utterance (Acts 2:4).

"And it shall be in the last days," God says, "that I will pour forth of My Spirit upon all mankind; and your sons and your daughters shall prophesy, and your young men shall see visions, and your old men shall dream dreams" (Acts 2:17).

And everyone kept feeling a sense of awe; and many wonders and signs were taking place through the apostles (Acts 2:43).

And seizing him by the right hand, he raised him up; and immediately his feet and his ankles were strengthened. And with a leap, he stood up and began to walk; and he entered the temple with them, walking and leaping and praising God... "And on the basis of faith in

*His name, it is the name of Jesus which has strength-
ened this man whom you see and know; and the faith
which comes through Him has given him this perfect
health in the presence of you all." (Acts 3:7,8,16).*

*And Stephen, full of grace and power, was performing
great wonders and signs among the people (Acts 6:8).*

*And the multitudes with one accord were giving atten-
tion to what was said by Philip, as they heard and saw
the signs, which he was performing. For in the case of
many who had unclean spirits, they were coming out
of them shouting with a loud voice; and many who
had been paralyzed and lame were healed. And there
was much rejoicing in that city (Acts 8:6-8).*

Peter raised Tabitha from the dead (Acts 9:36-42).

Note the events involved in the salvation of Cornelius and
his household: dialoguing with an angel in a vision (Acts
10:1-7); Peter's receiving instruction in a trance vision; divine serendipity (happy chance encounter brought about by
God - Acts 10:17,18); the Spirit speaking to Peter (Acts
10:19); a sermon which was interrupted by the Holy Spirit
falling upon the hearers and their beginning to speak in
tongues (Acts 10:34-46); and finally, water baptism (Acts
10:47,48).

Prophets foretold a worldwide famine, which came true
(Acts 11:27,28).

An angel appeared and freed Peter from prison (Acts 12:6-
11).

The word of the Lord came forth when prophets were in
prayer and fasting at Antioch (Acts 13:1-4).

Saul made Elymas the magician blind for a period of time
(Acts 13:8-12).

Signs and wonders were done at the hands of Paul (Acts
14:3).

Paul raised a lame man to his feet (Acts 14:8-10).

Paul got up and walked away after being stoned (Acts
14:19,20).

Paul cast a spirit of divination out of a slave-girl (Acts 16:16-18).

An earthquake opened the prison doors for Paul and Silas (Acts 16:25-33).

Paul prayed and laid hands on the Ephesian disciples and they received the Holy Spirit and began speaking in tongues (Acts 19:6).

God was doing extraordinary miracles by the hands of Paul, so that handkerchiefs or aprons were even carried from his body to the sick, and the diseases left them and the evil spirits went out (Acts 19:11,12).

Paul raised the dead (Acts 20:9-12).

Agabus prophesied (Acts 21:10,11).

A viper bit Paul and no harm came to him (Acts 28:3-5).

The manifestation of the Holy Spirit can be experienced through His gifts (I Cor. 12:7-11).

Tongues, knowledge and prophecy will be done away with when the perfect comes - (most likely a reference to the return of Christ, as knowledge is surely with us yet today - I Cor. 13:8-10).

We should earnestly desire spiritual gifts, especially to prophesy (I Cor. 14:1).

Paul said, "I wish that you all spoke in tongues but even more that you would prophesy" (I Cor. 14:5).

When we assemble, each one has a psalm, has a teaching, has a revelation, has a tongue, has an interpretation. Let all things be done for edification (I Cor. 14:26).

For we can all prophesy one by one (I Cor. 14:31).

The Christian understands the power God releases through His Church

The Lord said to my Lord, "Sit at My right hand, until I make Thine enemies a footstool for thy feet." There- fore let all the house of Israel know for certain that God has made Him both Lord and Christ - this Jesus Whom you crucified (Acts 2:34-36).

The Great Commission imparted the authority and the command to disciple all nations (Matt. 28:18-20).

Of the increase of His government there shall be no end - which means of the *decrease* of satan's government there shall be no end (Is. 9:7).

2

THE NEW AGE MOVEMENT: THE SPIRIT WITHOUT THE BIBLE

The New Age movement is such a wide and diverse movement that it is fairly difficult to characterize. However, we will see what we can do. You will find that its advocates seek after spiritual experiences, but they do not maintain the standard of the Bible.

Definition of the New Age

David Spangler, who has been lecturing and writing on the New Age for 25 years, defines New Age as "the condition that emerges when I live life in a creative, empowering, compassionate manner." ("The New Age Catalogue" by the editors of *Body Mind Spirit Magazine*, published by Doubleday, 1988. Introduction)

He also states, "I understand the New Age as a metaphor for being in the world in a manner that opens us to the presence of God - the presence of love and possibility - in the midst of our ordinariness." (Ibid. Introduction)

The ideals of the New Age are high and lofty and, if they can be achieved in even a small way by the power of man, they are tremendously enticing to a growing number of people. Therefore, people flock to read and study the literature put out by the New Age.

David Spangler goes on to say, "Inwardly, the New Age continues the historical effort of humanity to delve deeply into the mysteries of the nature of God, of ourselves, and of reality. In the midst of materialism, it is a rebirth of our sense of the sacred...The New Age is essentially a symbol representing the human heart and intellect in partnership with God building a better world that can celebrate values of community, wholeness and sacredness. It is a symbol for the emergence of social behavior based on a worldview that stimulates creativity, discipline, abundance and wholeness; it is a symbol for a more mature and unobstructed expression of the sacredness and love at the heart of life." (Ibid. Introduction)

The Eclectic Nature of the New Age

Since New Age followers are eclectic, they will draw from many sources, including the Bible and Christianity. For example, they have sought to make the rainbow their symbol, which, of course, is the sign of God's covenant promise that He would never destroy the earth again with a flood (Gen. 9:12-17). New Agers write on "centering," which is a word and an experience that has been used for decades by the Quaker church, and is described in Psalm 46:10. "The New Age Catalogue" even recommends the Christian book *Hinds Feet On High Places* by Hannah Hurnard published by Tyndale House Publishers, Inc. (Ibid. p. 89). Being eclectic, we should expect them to draw from Christianity as well as anyone else they desire. That does not concern Christians. Christians have a standard, the Word of God, and our acceptance of a truth is not based on whether or not a deceitful group has yet picked it up. We look to see if it is taught in Scripture (Acts 17:11).

Summary of a few of the New Age's basic tenets

1. **Who is God?** New Age does not believe in a personal God. Instead, its followers believe in a cosmic force they may call "The Evocative Other." This force permeates all things including matter, the animal kingdom, and man. This force is impersonal. It is something that one can tap into if

he takes the time and has the understanding of how to do so.

2. **What is the standard for truth?** New Age does not accept the Bible as a standard of infallible truth as the Christian does. He sees the Bible as a good book, but not one written by God. He sees truth as evolving and eclectic, so he seeks to draw together strands of truth from many different traditions.

3. **Who is Jesus Christ?** Jesus is not the Son of God in any special way, any more than we all are sons of God. Jesus was an enlightened teacher, whose teachings should be considered as one seeks out truth.

4. **What about salvation?** Salvation was not purchased with the blood of Jesus Christ, as Christians believe. Indeed, they believe that there is no such thing as an experience of salvation. Instead, there is an ongoing process of integration.

5. **Where do you focus?** On man and man's abilities. A Christian would focus instead on Jesus Christ and Christ's abilities flowing out through his heart and spirit. New Age focuses on connecting with the force of the "evocative other" and letting this force flow through.

6. **Where does wisdom come from?** For the Christian, wisdom comes from the Holy Spirit anointing the Scriptures, and the Holy Spirit granting direct dream, vision, and revelation into the believer's heart. For the New Ager, wisdom comes from man's search and from spiritual forces granting him experiences of insight.

7. **What stance does New Age take?** The Christian's stance is that man receives from God, and releases what he receives out to a hurting and needy world. The New Age stance is that man reaches to become god.

8. **The next age:** Christians believe that the future will be brought about by the working of God through His Church and by the return of Christ to rapture the Church. New Age believes that enlightened men will be the ones responsible for bringing about the next age.

9. **Intuitive development:** The Christian understands that God communicates directly Spirit-to-spirit with the Christian. The form this communication takes could fairly easily be called "intuition." **Webster's** defines intuition as "the immediate knowing of something without the conscious use of reasoning." That definition would surely take in knowing by the Spirit as taught in I Corinthians 2:10.

   But God hath revealed them unto us by his Spirit: for the Spirit searcheth all things, yea, the deep things of God.

   New Age believers have also discovered intuition. They realize it gives them access to spiritual knowledge and they seek to cultivate their intuitive abilities. However, a New Ager does not go into the spiritual world through Jesus Christ, so connections with evil spirits will be made as well as receipt of incorrect leading and messages through intuition. Correct leading may also occur, since God rains on the just and the unjust (Matt. 5:45).

10. **Contact with the S/spirit:** Christians believe in contact with the Holy Spirit through the Lord Jesus Christ. New Agers seek fellowship with any being in the spirit world. So, without the protection of being a born again Christian and going into the Spirit world using the name of the Lord Jesus Christ, they will connect to demons and evil spirits.

11. **Method of quieting yourself:** Christians often quiet themselves by coming into God's presence in worship while fixing their eyes on Jesus, the Author and Perfecter of their faith (Heb. 12:1,2). New Age followers will use a mantra, a nonsense syllable which, when repeated over and over, takes them into spirit-consciousness. This is a counterfeit of the biblical experience of speaking in tongues.

3

PHARISEEISM: THE BIBLE WITHOUT THE SPIRIT

The Pharisees accepted the Bible but rejected the Spirit. This underlying issue was at the core of much of the controversy they had with Jesus.

No spiritual discretion concerning sharing sensitive information

When requested, the Pharisees gave detailed, sensitive information to an evil state government which endangered Jesus and caused many babies to be killed (Matt. 2:1-6, 16-18).

They should have protected Jesus, even as Rahab protected the Jewish spies and was saved along with her household (Josh. 2). Instead, the Pharisees requested that the blood of Jesus be upon them and their children, which is exactly what they received in 70 A.D. when the Romans came and destroyed Jerusalem (Matt. 27:25).

The Maji heeded God's warning in a dream and did not give information to the evil state (Matt. 2:7-12). It appears the Maji, although not Jews (and thus not covenant children), had more spiritual insight than the Pharisees.

Emphasize the outer form of being right

The Pharisees wanted to look good by completing the right forms of worship (e.g., the baptism of John). However, John called them a brood of vipers and told them to bring forth fruit in keeping with repentance, and that, if their lives did not demonstrate good fruit, they would be cast out (Matt. 3:1-12).

Pharisees practice their righteousness (giving, prayer, fasting) before men to be noticed by them (Matt. 6:1-18).

Pharisees are nit-picking legalists. They put form before heart compassion, condemning eating and healing on the Sabbath (Matt. 12:1-14)

Pharisees devour widows' houses while making a pretense of long prayers. Therefore, they shall receive a greater condemnation (Matt. 23:14).

Pharisees travel widely in soul winning, but then make the convert twice as much a son of hell as they themselves are by teaching him legalism and traditions of men rather than how to move in the anointing of the Spirit of God (Matt. 23:15).

Pharisees are big on tithing but neglect weightier things such as justice, mercy and faithfulness (Matt. 23:23,24).

Pharisees don't care if the evidence before their eyes is a healed blind man. If the person who performed the healing has broken religious laws, as they understand them, then the healing and the healer are evil (Jn. 9:13-16).

Even the miracle of raising Lazarus after he had been dead four days was unacceptable to the Pharisees because they disagreed with Jesus' theology (Jn. 11:39-44). Therefore, they sought to kill Jesus (Jn. 11:46,53), as well as kill Lazarus because the evidence of his resurrection was causing people to believe on Jesus (Jn. 12:9-11).

Judgmental

Pharisees judge others without first judging themselves (Matt. 7:1-6).

Pharisees judge according to the flesh (Jn. 8:13,15).

Heart is evil, proud, jealous and lawless

"Not everyone who says to Me, 'Lord, Lord,' will enter the kingdom of heaven; but he who does the will of My Father Who is in heaven" and doesn't practice lawlessness (Matt. 7:21-23).

Pharisees take offense when the Holy Spirit's anointing rests upon someone in their midst, making him wiser and more effective than they (Matt. 13:53-57). Their offense diminishes the fruit of the anointing in their midst (Matt. 13:58).

Pharisees honor God with their speech, but their hearts are far away from God (Matt. 15:8).

Pharisees teach that people are to obey the Bible, and then don't obey it themselves (Matt. 23:2,3).

Pharisees focus on cleaning the outside, while the inside is full of robbery and self-indulgence, hypocrisy and lawlessness (Matt. 23:25:28).

No anointing is on their teaching

Pharisees teaching does not have the same authority as that of a Spirit-anointed teacher (Matt. 7:29).

Their eternal abode is hell

Sons of the kingdom may get cast out into the outer darkness; in that place there shall be weeping and gnashing of teeth (Matt. 8:12).

Religious people who see the miracles of God and do not repent will descend to Hades (Matt. 11:23).

Also, if you cause a little one who believes in Jesus to stumble, it is better for you that a heavy millstone be hung around your neck and that you be drowned in the depth of the sea (Matt. 18:6).

Repentant harlots will get into the kingdom of God before unrepentant Pharisees (Matt. 21:31,32).

The kingdom of God is taken away from Pharisees and given to a nation producing the fruit of it (Matt. 21:43).

Pharisees will go to hell (Matt. 23:33).

Condemn others whose actions or theology does not line up with what they believe is proper

Jesus was conceived in a way the Pharisees rejected, because He appeared to be an illegitimate child (Matt. 1:18). They insinuated He was born in fornication (Jn. 8:41).

When the Pharisees couldn't reconcile Jesus' actions with their theology, they decided He was an evil blasphemer (Matt. 9:2,3).

Pharisees complained that Jesus had fellowship with sinners (Matt. 9:11).

Come against those who have Spirit-empowered ministries

Pharisees said that Jesus cast out demons by the ruler of the demons (Matt. 9:34). Pharisees refuse to acknowledge that God is alive doing the supernatural. Religion demands that God's power be dead in the age in which the person is living.

Pharisees seek to discover ways to kill and destroy those who have Spirit-anointed ministries (Matt. 12:14).

Pharisees said that Jesus did His miracles by the power of satan (Matt. 12:24). Thus, they attribute Spirit-anointed ministries to the demonic or, in the 21st century, to New Agers.

Jesus said that if you speak against the Holy Spirit, you shall not be forgiven, either in this age, or in the age to come (Matt. 12:32). Pharisees today often attribute divine miracles to delusion, psychosomatic occurrences, and demonic and New Age manifestations. According to Matthew 12:32, they stand in danger of not being forgiven for this sin, as it is considered blasphemy against the Spirit (Matt. 12:31). Jesus said they shall be condemned by their words on the Day of Judgment (Matt. 12:36,37).

Pharisees question the authority of the Spirit-anointed minister (Matt. 21:23).

Pharisees call Spirit-anointed ministers demonized (Jn. 8:48).

The Pharisees listened to the teachings of a Spirit-anointed prophet and called Him insane and demonized (Jn. 10:20).

Pharisees will enter into secret agreements to attempt to destroy Spirit-anointed ministers (Acts 6:10-15).

Pharisees are stiff-necked (proud), uncircumcised in heart and ears (still have an evil heart), and are always resisting the Holy Spirit (always into rationalism and legalism, not spiritual Christianity - Acts 7:51).

But as at that time he who was born according to the flesh persecuted him who was born according to the Spirit, so it is now also. But what does the Scripture say? Cast out the bondwoman and her son, for the son of the bondwoman shall not be an heir with the son of the free woman. So then, brethren, we are not children of a bondwoman, but of the free woman (Gal. 4:29-31).

Pharisees kill the prophets and other righteous men (Matt. 23:29-36; see also Acts 7:52).

Pharisees were jealous of the crowds that followed Paul, so they began contradicting the things he said (Acts 13:45; 14:2; 17:5). They also incited the powers that be in the city to persecute Paul and drive him out of their district (Acts 13:49,50; 14:5).

Jews stoned Paul and left him for dead (Acts 14:19).

Their academic, theological training makes them wise in their minds, and often impoverished in their spirits

The things of the Spirit of God are hidden from the wise and intelligent and revealed to babes (Matt. 11:25).

The only way to know God is if you are given revelation of Him by His Son Jesus (Matt. 11:27). So, knowing God is a "revelation thing," not a rational "mental thing."

Jesus veiled His teaching by using parables so that those who had dull hearts would not hear and perceive and repent and be healed (Matt. 13:10-17).

God blinds the eyes and hardens the hearts of the Pharisees so they can't see or perceive and be converted and healed (Jn. 12:37-40).

Pharisees are blind guides of the blind. And if a blind man guides a blind man, both will fall into a pit (Matt 15:12-14; 23:16-22). Jesus said this because the Pharisees had no spiritual insight into the situation they were asking Jesus about, that is, the washing of hands when you eat bread (Matt. 15:1-14).

Pharisees interpret prophecy literally and miss the spiritual meaning in the prophecy. When the spiritual interpretation does manifest itself, they resist it (Matt. 17:10-12).

Pharisees try to test and trick with difficult theological questions (Matt. 19:3; 22:15-18,34,35).

Ask for a sign - while rejecting miracles

Pharisees resisted the miracles Jesus did, yet they tested Him, asking Him for a sign (Matt. 12:38,39, 16:1-4). Jesus would not give them one.

Remove vast sections of Scripture through their traditions

Pharisees invalidate the word of God for the sake of their traditions (Matt. 15:6).

Pharisees teach as doctrines the precepts of men (Matt. 15:9).

Pharisees shut off the way into the kingdom of heaven from men, and do not enter in themselves, nor do they allow those who are entering to go in (Matt. 23:13). (For example, they teach that there is no spirit world of dream, vision, miracles, deliverance, healing, etc.)

Jesus was protected by dreams and visions, things rejected by Pharisees (Matt. 1:19-25; 2:13-15, 19-23).

18

Love titles and approval of men

Pharisees like to exalt themselves by taking up positions of authority and by titles. Do not call people by titles (Matt. 23:2,6-12). Whoever exalts himself shall be humbled, and whoever humbles himself shall be exalted.

Pharisees love the approval of men rather than the approval of God (Jn. 12:43).

They are of the devil

Pharisees cannot understand because they cannot hear, because they are of the devil (Jn. 8:43-47).

Pharisees are not Jesus' sheep, and do not hear His voice. Jesus' sheep hear His voice (Jn. 10:26,27).

Satan uses Scripture, so using Scripture does not prove you are a Christian (Matt. 4:1-11).

Have a negative worldview

Jesus concludes His debate with the Pharisees in Matthew 5-7 by saying that the gate is small and the way narrow that leads to life and few are those who find it (Matt. 7:13,14). I assume He was talking about the gate for the Pharisees and the number of Pharisees who will repent and make it to heaven.

Since Pharisees do not believe that the power of God is active in their generation, and they do believe that the power of satan is active in their generation, they believe for the take-over of the planet by satan rather than by God.

4

Distinguishing Traits of Christianity, the New Age Movement, and Phariseeism

What are some of the key traits of Christianity, the New Age movement and Phariseeism? Christianity and Phariseeism are both defined quite clearly in the Bible. Our definition of the New Age movement will come from my current understanding of who they are. I have read an overview book written by one of their leaders in an effort to gain a perspective of how they would define themselves.

Some Distinguishing Traits of Christianity

1. Believes God rules the universe.

2. Believes God rules in the realm of mankind.

3. Believes God is the same yesterday, today and forever.

4. Believes the Bible is the inspired Word of God, and that it can be applied quite directly to our lives.

5. Rejects any traditions of men negating the power of God.

6. Believes the Holy Spirit is joined to the believer's spirit and divine anointing flows out through the heart of the believer.

7. Believes in revelation knowledge rather than rationalism.

Some Distinguishing Traits of the New Age Movement

1. Believes the Evocative Other rules the universe.

2. Believes man creates his own destiny.

3. Believes God is a force to be used for man's own desires.

4. Believes the Bible is simply a nice book.

5. Believes man can be empowered by connecting to the Evocative Other.

6. Believes the force of the universe is present in everything.

7. Believes there is a wisdom man can receive from "the force."

Some Distinguishing Traits of Phariseeism

1. Believes God rules the universe.

2. Believes satan rules in the realm of mankind.

3. Believes God's power is quite limited in the Church age.

4. Believes the Bible is the inspired Word of God, however, most of it doesn't apply directly to our lives.

5. Teaches many traditions of men limiting God's power in this dispensation.

6. Believes Christ lives in the heart of the believer, but ignores or rejects the power of the Holy Spirit.

7. Believes God gave man a mind and he is supposed to use it (rationalism).

Some Distinguishing Traits of Christianity

1. Believes God rules the universe. The Bible calls Him King of Kings and Lord of Lords (I Tim. 6:15; Rev. 17:14; 19:16). That not only makes God politically active; it makes Him the foremost Ruler in the world of politics. God is called Almighty God (Gen. 17:1), the Creator of the universe (Gen. 1-2), the Sustainer of the universe (Col. 1:17), and He will be the Culminator of the universe when His Son Jesus returns for His Church. This will be followed by the great white throne judgment (Rev. 20:11-15), and an eternal abode in heaven with Him for those who have made Jesus Christ their Lord and Savior.

2. Believes God rules in the realm of mankind. Daniel said over and over, "The Most High rules in the realm of mankind" (e.g., Dan. 4:17). Jesus obviously demonstrated this rule as He released God's power into the world He touched. He delivered people from demonic bondage, sickness and even death (Acts 10:38). God's active rule in the affairs of this earth is clearly shown by the fact that God cares for us, to the extent that He even numbers the hairs on our heads (Matt. 10:30), and has instructed us to pray for Him to meet our daily needs so that He can provide them for us (Matt. 6:25-34). The Bible says God oversees the events of this world and works all things after the counsel of His will (Eph. 1:11). God works all things together for good to them that love Him and are called according to His purpose (Rom. 8:28).

3. Believes God is the same yesterday, today and forever. The Bible teaches that Jesus Christ is the same yesterday, today, and forever (Heb. 13:8). He gave dream and vision from Genesis to Revelation and declares He will continue to do so in the last days (Acts 2:17). Jesus healed all that were oppressed (Matt. 4:23,24) and sent His disciples out with the commission to preach the gospel, speak with new tongues, and lay hands on the sick (Mk. 16:15-18). Jesus demonstrated God's power completely in His life. Jesus is our Example Whom we are to follow (I Pet. 2:21).

4. Believes the Bible is the inspired Word of God, and that it can be applied quite directly to our lives. "All Scripture is given by inspiration of God, and is profitable for doctrine, for reproof, for correction, for instruction in righteousness; that the man of God may be perfect, thoroughly furnished unto all good works" (II Tim. 3:16,17). The Bible was written to provide us examples of how we are to live (I Cor. 10:11). We are not to view it as a lifestyle unattainable to us, but rather a lifestyle we can and are called to demonstrate. The Bible is to be lived, not simply read. Jesus did fulfill the ceremonial law in His life, death and resurrection. But with the exception of what Jesus fulfilled, the rest of the Law and the Bible is still in effect today (Matt. 5:17-20).

5. Rejects any traditions of men negating the power of God. Jesus refuted the Pharisees who invalidated the word of God for the sake of their traditions (Matt. 15:6). Jesus demonstrated God's power in their midst by healing the sick, casting out demons, and raising the dead (Matt. 10:8; 11:5). However, the Pharisees were so committed to their traditions that they considered removing the evidence of Jesus' mighty miracles, by putting Lazarus back to death, so there would be no proof that Jesus had raised him from the dead. Pharisees will not listen to reason. Pharisees will not be swayed by circumstances of God's power surrounding them and staring them straight in the face, for their theological prejudices and necklace of pride keep them from recognizing the living Lord in their midst. In fact, they think they do God a favor by killing the prophets God sends to them (Acts 7:51-60). Christians, on the other hand, know that they must never hold to a form of godliness while denying the power thereof, and that they should not associate with those who practice such things (II Tim. 3:5).

6. Believes the Holy Spirit is joined to the believer's spirit and divine anointing flows out through the heart of the believer. The Bible makes it clear that when the Lord Jesus Christ is invited into life as Lord and Savior, the convert becomes "one Spirit with Him" (I Cor. 6:17). God is joined to the spirit, and Christians become partakers of the divine nature (II Pet.1: 4). Jesus said that the indwelling Holy Spirit is sensed as "flow" - out of your innermost being shall flow rivers of living water; this He spoke of the Spirit (Jn. 7:37-39). So the Christian learns to die to self's efforts and become alive and sensitive to the "flow" experience of the Spirit of God within him (Gal. 2:20). To put it another way, it is learning to walk and live in the Spirit (Gal. 5:25). The Christian lives out of the God Who lives within and lives tuned to flow, keeping the eyes fixed on Jesus (Heb. 12:1,2).

7. Believes in revelation knowledge rather than rationalism. The Bible makes it clear that our thoughts are not God's thoughts and our ways are not His ways (Is. 55:8). "For as the heavens are higher than the earth, so are My ways higher than your ways, and My thoughts than your thoughts" (Is. 55:9). Therefore, if we live out of our reason, we will not be living out of God, because His ways are so much different than our reason. His ways demand faith, which is born in revelation knowledge. Reason, on the other hand, is born in the mind's abilities and limitations. Abraham, the father of faith, became a great man of faith because he believed the revelation of God to him in a dream/vision that he would be the father of a multitude (Gen. 12:1-3; 15:1-6). Jesus said He lived out of divine initiative rather than reason (Is. 11:3; Jn. 5:19,20,30). The Bible nowhere encourages us to reason or to live out of our reason.

Actually, the only command concerning reason in the entire Bible is, "Come now, and let us reason together, saith the LORD: though your sins be as scarlet, they shall be as white as snow; though they be red like crimson, they shall be as wool" (Is. 1:18). So we are only encouraged to reason if we are doing it **together with God,** and according to the example of that verse, our reasoning will involve picturing ("though your sins be as scarlet, they shall be as white as snow"). Most westerners would not consider picturing to be reasoning at all. They consider reasoning an analytical, cognitive function centering in the revolving of ideas around in the mind. God nowhere endorses such a process in the Bible; moreover, many times He comes against those who did reason in this way (Matt. 16:5-12; Mk. 2:5-12; Lk. 5:21,22).

Rationalism is a false god that is worshiped by the western world, even by many western "Christians." The Bible is clear from cover to cover that God wants us to live out of revelation knowledge from His voice and vision flowing from within our hearts.

Some Distinguishing Traits of the New Age Movement

1. Believes the Evocative Other rules the universe. New Agers do not believe that God is a personal God. Instead, they believe in a force to be tapped into. They have reduced God from a Person to simply one of His attributes, which is that He is almighty and powerful. However, the true God is much more than simply might and power. He is love, also. He is a Being Who is to be loved, honored, revered and worshiped.

2. Believes man creates his own destiny. Man has tremendous abilities which, when properly harnessed and released, will allow the New Age believer to excel and even evolve to higher and higher planes. Destiny is directly related to drawing out of inner capacities. One can overcome surroundings (even if negative and evil) by drawing from the force within. These beliefs surely have some parallels to what the Bible teaches is a possible lifestyle for the Spirit-filled believer. However, the Spirit-filled believer changes his life by drawing upon the power of the Holy Spirit within.

3. Believes God is a force to be used for man's own desires. This force permeates all matter (which, of course, is true in that the power of God does permeate all matter and even is the Force that holds all matter together - Col. 1:17). However, New Agers do not realize that God is much more than a force. He is a personal God with Whom you must establish a personal relationship by inviting Him into your heart and spirit through repentance and prayer. They do not recognize that the blood of Jesus cleanses sins and the Holy Spirit grants access before the throne of God (I Jn.1: 9, Eph. 2:18). So yes, the force of God permeating the universe can be accessed; however, God's protocol is establishing a personal relationship with Jesus Christ as Lord and Savior before trying to access this power. This protects from demonic counterfeits.

4. Believes the Bible is simply a nice book. New Agers do not believe that the Bible is the inspired words of God to mankind. They do not believe that all their spiritual experiences should be brought to the Bible and tested against the spiritual experiences which people in the Bible had and against the laws and commandments found in Scripture. So, New Age believers are left without a standard. The Christian has a standard to gauge experiences against. It is the Bible.

5. Believes man can be empowered by connecting to the Evocative Other. If the Evocative Other is the force of God present in the universe, then it is true that man can and will be empowered by being connected to Him. However, New Age followers fail to see that this Evocative Other is the God of the Bible, Who has specific moral commands and procedures to be carefully followed if you want to enter the world of spiritual forces safely. The New Ager will encourage centering down, which is quite similar to the Bible's command to "be still and know that I am God" (Ps. 46:10). However, the role of Jesus will be missed in the whole equation, thus placing followers of this practice at the mercy of evil spirits.

6. Believes the force of the universe is present in everything. This indeed is true, as the Bible specifically states that God is all and in all (Col. 1:17). So the force and power of God is the glue that holds the atoms and molecules together, and when He ceases to do this, the elements will melt with a fervent heat (II Pet. 3:10). However, what they fail to realize is that God is more than a force. He is a Being of love and mercy and forgiveness. He will forgive their sins and cleanse them through the blood of His Son, Jesus Christ, which was shed for their sins at Calvary, if they will just repent and turn away from their sin, and invite Jesus to come into their hearts as their Master and Savior.

7. Believes there is a wisdom man can receive from "the force." That is true, if God is the Force of the universe, which He surely is, since He is Almighty God (Gen. 17:1). That means all might comes from God. It is also biblical that God is more than might. He is the Spirit of wisdom and understanding and knowledge (Is. 11:2). So yes, when the power of God is touched, the wisdom of God is touched. Again, though, if not a born again Christian, and under the covering of Jesus' blood, the New Ager, when entering the spiritual realm, opens up to the Holy Spirit and to any and all spirits. It is likely New Agers will come into contact with evil spirits bringing destruction to their lives. The only safe way to pursue the spiritual world is as a born again Holy Spirit-filled Christian.

Some Distinguishing Traits of Phariseeism

1. Believes God rules the universe. They would express the same belief as Christianity, as delineated in number one above, with the exception that they do not like to think of God as being politically active, as that would lend credence to the fact that they, too, should be politically active. Instead, they tend to teach that Christians should be uninvolved in politics (and Hollywood, etc.).

2. Believes satan rules in the realm of mankind. Satan is considered the prince of the power of the air (Eph. 2:2). Thus, they believe that satan rules over planet Earth bringing all sorts of sickness, death and destruction.

3. Believes God's power is quite limited in the Church age. God was powerful in the Old Testament. God was powerful in the Gospels. God was powerful in the book of Acts, and God will be powerful in the future when He returns to set up His kingdom. However, in the Church age, God has chosen to limit His power because now we have the Bible at our fingertips. My question is, why, if the Church age is the grand consummation of God's redemptive plan for mankind here on earth, would He choose to make it the time when His power is most limited? If He defeated satan at Calvary, and commissioned the Church to disciple all nations, and empowered Her to do this with signs following (Mk. 16:17), why would we say that there will be no signs following? It just doesn't make sense to me.

4. Believes the Bible is the inspired Word of God, however, most of it doesn't apply directly to our lives. There are several approaches currently in use to remove the Bible from people's lives. One approach is Dispensation. Dispensationalists claim that the Old Testament was for the Jews, the Gospels describe Jesus' life, the book of Acts was transitional, and the book of Revelation is for the future. The part of the Bible that "may" be applicable to our lives is the New Testament letters. Even with these, one must take into consideration the customs of the times, and the fact that the letters were written to select groups of people and not directly to you and me.

5. Teaches many traditions of men limiting God's power in this dispensation. Like the Pharisees of Jesus' day who negated the power of God through their traditions, the Pharisees of today also negate the power of God through their twenty-first century traditions (Matt. 15:6). The two primary traditions espoused today are dispensationalism and demythalization. Dispensationalism claims that God doesn't do mighty works of power anymore in the Church age because now we have the Bible. Demythalizationists remove the power of God by saying it wasn't really there in the first place and that the recorded miracles were simply myths. So from the most conservative fundamentalist to the most raging liberal, all are equally convinced that God's power is not present to touch people's lives in this age. The Pharisees in the first century would not accept the Jesus' miracles they saw right in front of their eyes. So today, Pharisees will not accept the many miracles occurring right in front of their eyes. Instead, they call them demonic manifestations, delusions, or deceptions. What they must note is that the Bible strictly cautions us against calling good, evil (Is. 5:20).

6. Believes Christ lives in the heart of the believer, but ignores or rejects the power of the Holy Spirit. Pharisees are big on the formal prayer of inviting Jesus into the heart, but they go on to stress that you need not "feel" anything, because feelings are soulish. Obviously, this misses entirely the reality mentioned in Romans 8:16, "The Spirit Himself **bears witness** with our spirit that we are children of God." (Wouldn't you say that "bearing witness" is a feeling of some sort? I certainly would.) Since Pharisees are so against feelings and emotions of any kind, they would never subscribe to living out of "flow" (Jn. 7:37-39), or letting an emotion guide their lives and actions. However, Jesus did. "Jesus...was **moved** with **compassion** toward them, and He healed their sick" (Matt. 14:14). In addition, Jesus did nothing on His own initiative, but only those things He saw or heard the Father doing (Jn. 5:19,20,30). So, contrary to the life of a Pharisee, Jesus lived out of the flow of the Holy Spirit within Him.

7. Believes God gave man a mind and he is supposed to use it (rationalism). This statement is made so commonly that few in the twenty-first century western world would even question its validity. Of course, God gave you a mind in order for you to use it. You are to study with it and reason with it. However, study and reason are not encouraged in the Bible. Admittedly, the King James Version of the Bible says, "*Study* to show yourselves approved..." (II Tim. 2:15). However, if you will examine the Greek behind this word, you will find that it should be translated "be diligent" rather than "study." The New American Standard Bible accurately translates it "be diligent" in this verse, and the word "study" is not found even once in the NASB.

God did not give us minds to use. He gave us minds to do with what He has commanded us to do with every other part of our bodies - that is, to present them to Him as living sacrifices so He can use them and flow through them with the anointing of His Holy Spirit (Rom. 12:1). I am to learn to present my mind to God to use. In doing that, I present it to the "flow" of the Holy Spirit within me (Jn. 7:37-39). I fix my eyes on Jesus and tune to flow (Heb. 12:2). I let this divine flow guide the reasoning process, and then I receive what I call anointed reasoning. Luke 1:1-3 demonstrates the process and results of anointed reason.

Summary: The purpose of this chapter is to help to clearly see what the Bible teaches concerning the basic underlying tenets of Christianity, and two counterfeits, the New Age and Phariseeism. Hopefully, you discovered that you are a participant in Christianity and not either of the other cults described. If you find levels of Phariseeism within yourself, don't despair and don't attack. The solution is simple. Repent and God will save you. I grew up in Phariseeism. When I discovered many traits of Phariseeism in myself, I repented and asked God's forgiveness and healing and restoration, which He graciously gave to me. If pride wells up and you seek to attack and destroy me, that will be the crowning proof that you, indeed, are a Pharisee, because Pharisees carry the spirit of murder with them. They murdered Jesus, right along with all the prophets God sent to them (Acts 7:51-60). So I pray for your sake that you repent rather than attack. If you kill me, I just get to go to heaven sooner. However, I wouldn't want to be you when you stand before the great white throne of God on Judgment Day. Because if, indeed, you are a Pharisee and not a Christian, Jesus clearly said that you are of satan, which means you will not go to heaven (Jn. 8:43-47). That would be tragic for you.

After reading this chapter have you decided you are a New Ager? Would you like to know what God would have you do so you can safely move into the spiritual world and connect with His Holy Spirit and not evil spirits? Appendix A shows the steps of a prayer to invite Jesus Christ into your heart and life as your Lord and Savior.

Additional resources: The book *Surprised by the Power of the Spirit* by Jack Deere is the story of one evangelical theologian's journey from believing that miracles were not for this age (dispensationalism), to realizing that indeed they are for today. If you need an excellent, clearly thought out theology of why you should move from a belief that the age of miracles has past to a belief that the age of miracles is still with us, read this book. Need more?

How Do You Know? by Mark and Patti Virkler for an examination of 5500 verses supporting this truth.

5

FEAR, FAITH, AND A POSITIVE MENTAL ATTITUDE

Faith and fear are both essentially spirits. One has either a spirit of faith or a spirit of fear. This spirit will tend to permeate all ideas, attitudes, and actions of the person.

I was converted because of a spirit of fear. I did not want to go to hell. I was trained up as a new Christian to fear the antichrist and the takeover of this world by the antichrist's strategies, which included a one-world government and demonic Illuminati. Thus, the spirit of fear was deepened within me. My ideas, attitudes, and actions were all controlled by the fear that gripped me. I was taught to separate myself from the world, to buy a self-sufficient house in the hills, to lay up food for the coming calamity, and to be willing to starve since I would not take the mark of the beast. I believed the Church would be ravaged by the antichrist. Of course, I had Scriptures to back up every aspect of my spirit of fear.

I have now come to realize that fear is as powerful as faith. Fear is actually faith in reverse, and everything faith can accomplish, fear can accomplish. However, fear accomplishes it toward the building of the kingdom of darkness, while faith accomplishes it toward the building of the Kingdom of God.

Christianity and Faith	The New Age Movement and a Positive Mental Attitude	Phariseeism and Faith in the Antichrist (Fear)
1. Believes God disciples the world through His Church.	1. Believes you choose your own destiny (which is determined by what you place your faith in).	1. Believes the Church will live in fear and defeat until She is snatched out in the rapture.
2. Believes satan was defeated at Calvary and the Church is now involved in a "mopping up campaign."	2. Believes in a generalized force of evil and a generalized force of good, and that the world is moving toward the good.	2. Believes satan still rules this world, and will drive the Church underground.
3. Receives God's Word that His children are more than conquerors.	3. Believes a positive mental attitude will create a positive lifestyle.	3. Receives the idea that God's children are the underdog.
4. Sees a vision of God's enemies becoming His footstool.	4. Sees a vision of goodness prevailing.	4. Sees a vision of God's enemies becoming more and more powerful in the world.
5. Speaks in faith that righteousness will overcome wickedness.	5. Believes only positive words should be spoken.	5. Speaks in faith that wickedness will overcome righteousness.
6. Acts in faith extending the Kingdom of God throughout the earth.	6. Acts in faith upon the vision that goodness will prevail.	6. Acts in faith (in satan's power) as they retreat into a cloistered religious sub-culture or into the mountains to hide from the coming desolation.
7. Believes for and experiences an overcoming lifestyle of "promised land" blessings.	7. Believes for and experiences a fairly positive lifestyle (because the Bible says, "According to your faith, be it unto you").	7. Believes for and experiences a fairly negative lifestyle (because the Bible says, "According to your faith, be it unto you").

Christianity and Faith

1. Believes God disciples the world through His Church.

And Jesus came and spake unto them, saying, "All power is given unto me in heaven and in earth. Go ye therefore, and teach [disciple] all nations..." (Matt. 28:18,19 KJV).

The verse should read, "disciple all nations" (as translated in the NASB), not "teach all nations" (as translated in the KJV). The Greek verb meaning "disciple" is a form of *mathetes*, which is translated "disciple" more than 250 times in the KJV Bible and only twice translated "teach." Matthew 28:19 is one of these two unfortunate mis-translations. The Greek word for "teach" is actually *didasko* and is used in Matthew 28:20.

The Bible clearly says that Jesus commissioned and empowered the Church to disciple all nations, that is, to bring them under the discipline of the Lord.

2. Believes satan was defeated at Calvary and the Church is now involved in a "mopping up campaign."

When Jesus rose from the grave, He defeated the forces of satan and took the keys of death and hell from him (Rev. 1:18). Satan's authority was ripped from him, ALL things were put in subjection under Jesus' feet, and Jesus was made head over ALL things (Eph. 1:20-23). Then the Church was raised up with Jesus and seated in Him in heavenly places to display the power, riches, and kindness of God toward us in Christ Jesus (Eph. 2:5-8).

The Bible is true: "Of the increase of His government there shall be no end," which means satan's government must be continuously decreasing (Is. 9:7)!

3. Receives God's Word that His children are more than conquerors.

"And they overcame him by the blood of the Lamb, and by the word of their testimony..." (Rev. 12:11). The Church's faith in the work accomplished by the blood of Jesus, and Her willingness to testify in faith concerning the promises of God to Her, will cause Her to receive, through the anointing of the Holy Spirit, the power and provision and authority and dominion which God has promised and given Her (Mk. 11:22-24). See also Romans 8:37 and I John 5:4.

4. Sees a vision of God's enemies becoming His footstool. The Bible says that Jesus will sit at the right hand of God in heaven UNTIL God makes His enemies a footstool for His feet (Acts 2:34,35). So, once the Church accomplishes the Great Commission, Christ is returning to earth. Without a vision, the people perish (Prov. 29:18). God has given the Church a powerful vision of Her making His enemies His footstool by discipling every nation! How's that for a positive vision and eschatology of victory?

5. Speaks in faith that righteousness will overcome wickedness. "Truly I say to you, whoever says to this mountain, `Be taken up and cast into the sea,' and does not doubt in his heart, but believes that what he says is going to happen, it shall be granted him" (Mk. 11:23 NASB). "According to your faith be it unto you" (Matt. 9:29). "All things are possible to those that believe" (Mk. 9:23). "For the earth will be filled with the knowledge of the glory of the Lord, as the waters cover the sea" (Hab. 2:14 NASB). "The people which sat in darkness saw great light; and to them which sat in the region and shadow of death light is sprung up" (Matt. 4:16). "Again, a new commandment I write unto you, which thing is true in him and in you: because the darkness is past, and the true light now shineth" (I Jn. 2:8).

6. Acts in faith extending the Kingdom of God throughout the earth. Christians attack the forces of darkness, dispelling them and replacing them with the Kingdom of God (Eph. 5:8,9).

When light enters a room, darkness must flee. When Christians enter an area, darkness must flee. That is why Christians are to enter each and every area of society and speak in faith, letting the light of Christ radiate out through them and dispel the darkness (Dan. 12:3; Matt. 5:14-16).

7. Believes for and experiences an overcoming lifestyle of "promised land" blessings. The Israelites who fought in faith possessed the Promised Land of milk and honey, built homes there, and lived in the blessings of God (Josh. 1-13). This is an example for us to follow (I Cor. 10:1-11). Those who will battle in faith, obeying God's voice, and believing in His power and anointing to flow through them, will receive what they fight for as well.

The New Age Movement and a Positive Mental Attitude

1. Believes you choose your own destiny (which is determined by what you place your faith in). Each has the opportunity to make of life exactly what he wants to make of it. By believing in negatives one can have a negative lifestyle. By believing in positives, a positive lifestyle can be had. The choice is up to the New Age follower.

2. Believes in a generalized force of evil and a generalized force of good, and that the world is moving toward the good. There is no literal heaven or hell. However, New Agers believe in moving toward increased light in life and applying the mind to learning and obeying the right principles.

3. Believes a positive mental attitude will create a positive lifestyle. New Agers get exactly what they believe for. Therefore, believing for a positive lifestyle causes a positive lifestyle.

4. Sees a vision of goodness prevailing. New Agers see the evolutionary process causing the world to become a better and better place in which to live. They believe the more you look upon this vision, the more you will be drawn into it.

5. Believes you should only speak positive words. New Agers believe that spoken words control your destiny. If negative words are spoken, negative experiences will occur. If positive words are spoken, there will be positive experiences. Words are creative forces.

6. Acts in faith upon the vision that goodness will prevail. New Agers lend their lives to making the world a better place doing the things they understand will contribute to the betterment of the earth and civilization.

7. Believes for and experiences a fairly positive lifestyle (because the Bible says, "According to your faith, be it unto you"). The biblical principle of faith works for anyone who wants to work it, whether a Christian, a New Ager or a Pharisee. Faith is a universal law, and the components of faith (seeing, pondering, speaking and acting) work for all who will work them.

Phariseeism and Faith in the Antichrist (Fear)

1. Believes the Church will live in fear and defeat until She is snatched out in the rapture. Believes that the world will get worse and worse, evil will become stronger and stronger, and the Church will be persecuted and driven underground by the antichrist. Just before She is totally extinguished, the few who have remained righteous will be snatched out in the rapture.

2. Believes satan still rules this world, and will drive the Church underground. Believes that satan is powerful. Evil is powerful. The antichrist is powerful, and the Church will be at his mercy. The Church will not take the mark of the beast so believers will not be able to buy or sell and will be driven into hiding. Many will likely starve or be tortured and killed.

3. Receives the idea that God's children are the underdog. The Church does not lead in society. The Church is to withdraw Herself from an evil and wicked generation. You are aliens to this world and your citizenship is in heaven. Therefore you should not even try to have a godly influence in the lives of those you touch.

4. Sees a vision of God's enemies becoming more and more powerful in the world. The antichrist will bring forth a one-world government. It will control the international money supply and the armies and the food. All will be forced to obey it or suffer death, unless they flee and hide.

5. Speaks in faith that wickedness will overcome righteousness. Speaks forth with power and persuasiveness this horrendous and negative worldview of satan engulfing the world in his mighty claws. Declares this view in books, sermons, movies, tracts, etc.

6. Acts in faith (in satan's power) as they retreat into a cloistered religious sub-culture or into the mountains to hide from the coming desolation. Encourages one to flee and hide from the wrath to come, to purchase a farm in the mountains for survival when the world as it is known collapses.

7. Believes for and experiences a fairly negative lifestyle (because the Bible says, "According to your faith, be it unto you"). Pharisees are at odds with much of society, and with anyone who would dare to be positive in the midst of such a horrific world. Pharisees constantly speak, see and act in a negative fashion, so they draw the world's worst to themselves.

Summarizing - The Church, the New Age and Phariseeism: The Church is positive because it believes that the power of the Holy Spirit will work through Her to transform the earth. The New Age is positive, because they have learned to utilize several of the biblical principles concerning how faith works. Pharisees are extremely negative, because they are using all the principles of faith in reverse. They believe in satan's power rather than God's power in this present age. They speak of the works of the antichrist, rather than the works of the risen Christ. They set their eyes on the antichrist, rather than fixing their eyes on Jesus (Heb. 12:2). They act in faith in satan's power rather than acting in faith in God's power. And, of course, they interpret the Bible in such a way as to proof-text their negativity. There are plenty of verses used to do that.

A large group of people that are believing for the takeover of the world by satan are Pharisees! This is startling. You would think that the biggest group should be the satanic church, but its numbers are small in comparison to the number of Pharisees on the planet. It's easier now to see why satan works overtime ensuring that many who seek after Christianity actually become Pharisees and are filled with doctrines of demons. Pharisees most likely advance satan's kingdom more than any other group on earth.

Obviously, you can find Scripture verses to back up certain views of both the cult of the New Age and the cult of Phariseeism. That is because in order for it to be a good counterfeit, it must have some truth mixed in with the error. However, it still contains error. Their spirit and their foundations are wrong. Pharisees start out with more faith in satan's power to affect the world than they have faith in the power of the risen Christ to affect the world. The New Agers don't start with a personal God Who died on the cross to save them from their sin. So both are fundamentally flawed, which means that regardless of any pieces of truth that they may have, their super-structures are being built upon faulty foundations.

Thought: "Leadership is automatically transferred to those who remain optimistic."

6

GIFTS OF THE HOLY SPIRIT VERSUS ESP

Christianity and the Gifts of the Holy Spirit

1. Believes the gifts of the Holy Spirit are for today.

2. Believes the gifts of the Holy Spirit release the power of God through anointed individuals to a hurting and needy world.

3. Believes you are to seek spiritual gifts.

4. Believes you are to glorify God when the gifts of the Holy Spirit are operated.

The New Age Movement and Extra Sensory Perception

1. Believes ESP is available to all.

2. Believes ESP allows you access to spiritual abilities.

3. Believes you are to seek to operate ESP.

4. Believes ESP is a natural ability everyone has, thus the operation of ESP glorifies self.

Phariseeism and the Gifts of the Holy Spirit

1. Believes the gifts of the Holy Spirit ceased when the Bible was written.

2. Believes the gifts of the Holy Spirit were to prove to the world that Christianity was real.

3. Believes you are not to seek the gifts of the Holy Spirit.

4. Believes the so-called "gifts of the Holy Spirit" are actually demonic, and thus glorify satan.

Christianity and the Gifts of the Holy Spirit

1. Believes the gifts of the Holy Spirit are for today. God is the same yesterday, today and forever (Heb. 13:8). The Church was commissioned to heal the sick (Mk. 16:17,18). In the book of James we are encouraged to anoint the sick with oil and pray for them and they shall be healed (Jas. 5:14-16).

2. Believes the gifts of the Holy Spirit release the power of God through anointed individuals to a hurting and needy world. The gifts of the Holy Spirit are to be used to build up the body of Christ (I Cor. 12:7; 14:4). "When you assemble, each one has a psalm, has a teaching, has a revelation, has a tongue, has an interpretation. Let all things be done for edification" (I Cor. 14:26 NASB). "Tongues are for a sign...to unbelievers; but prophecy is for a sign...to those who believe" (I Cor. 14:22 NASB).

3. Believes you are to seek spiritual gifts. "Therefore, my brethren, desire earnestly to prophesy, and do not forbid to speak in tongues" (I Cor. 14:39 NASB). "Pursue love, yet desire earnestly spiritual gifts, but especially that you may prophesy" (I Cor. 14:1 NASB).

4. Believes you are to glorify God when the gifts of the Holy Spirit are operated. When Paul and Barnabas healed a lame man, the people of Lystra called them gods. However Paul quickly rebuked them and said the glory must go to the true God and not to them (Acts 14:8-18).

The New Age Movement and Extra Sensory Perception

1. Believes ESP is available to all. ESP is an ability that all humans have. It is a natural ability, which can be developed.

2. Believes ESP allows you access to spiritual abilities. ESP can allow access to the spiritual world and to spiritual forces. Thus, connecting them to spirit world forces can enhance abilities.

3. Believes you are to seek to operate ESP. There are many places to go to learn to develop ESP abilities. ESP has been carefully tested in scientific studies, and scientific learning experiences have been designed to help people develop their ESP abilities.

4. Believes ESP is a natural ability everyone has, thus the operation of ESP glorifies self. Since man is the originator of this ability, man receives the glory by using it.

Phariseeism and the Gifts of the Holy Spirit

1. Believes the gifts of the Holy Spirit ceased when the Bible was written. When that which was perfect came (i.e., the Bible) the gifts of the Holy Spirit were no longer needed. This argument is built upon a very poor and inaccurate interpretation of I Corinthians 13:10. The Bible does not define "the perfect which is coming" as the Bible. It would more likely be defined as the return of Jesus Christ. (See also I Corinthians 13:12.)

2. Believes the gifts of the Holy Spirit were to prove to the world that Christianity was real. Initially the gifts were necessary to prove to the world that Christianity was real. However, now they are no longer necessary. I believe that each new generation needs to have it proven to them afresh and anew that Christianity is real.

3. Believes you are not to seek the gifts of the Holy Spirit. "You are to seek the Giver rather than the gifts" is a refrain often heard. However, the Bible says, "Seek ye the Lord AND HIS STRENGTH" (Ps. 105:4). So the Bible doesn't say one and not the other. The Bible says seek BOTH, God *and* His power.

4. Believes the so-called "gifts of the Holy Spirit" are actually demonic, and thus glorify satan. This is based on Matthew 7:21-23, where it says that those who prophesied and cast out demons and did many miracles will be told by Jesus, "Depart from Me, you who practice lawlessness." I think a better point to take from this verse is that if you are lawless (do not obey God's moral law), then regardless of the operation of the gifts in your life, you are not God's child.

44

Summary: Christians seek to experience the gifts of the Holy Spirit. New Agers seek to experience ESP. Pharisees do not seek ongoing, direct contact with the Living God, and call those who do seek and experience such, either New Agers or demonized. Jesus sought such and was told by the Pharisees that He cast out demons by Beelzebul (Matt. 12:24). Nothing has changed in 2000 years.

7

DREAMS

Dreams defined: An inner flow of pictures while one is asleep.

Christianity and Dreams

1. Believes God grants dreams.

2. Asks God for dreams in faith.

3. Seeks God's interpretation of dreams he receives.

4. Receives God's wisdom through dreams.

5. Receives God's direction and faith through dreams.

6. Acts in faith upon his dreams.

7. Worships God for the dreams He gives.

The New Age Movement and Dreams

1. Believes dreams come from the heart and spirit world.

2. Seeks dreams.

3. Seeks to interpret own dreams or seeks the help of other people.

4. Receives limited insight through dreams.

5. Receives some direction and faith through dreams.

6. May act upon dreams.

7. Is thankful for what dreams teach.

Phariseeism and Dreams

1. Generally views dreams as leftover, undigested food.

2. Doesn't ask God for dreams.

3. Doesn't seek any interpretation of dreams.

4. Doesn't receive any wisdom through dreams.

5. Doesn't receive any direction or faith through dreams.

6. Doesn't act in faith upon his dreams.

7. Doesn't worship God for the gift of dreams.

Christianity and Dreams

1. Believes God grants dreams.

And he said, "Hear now my words: If there be a prophet among you, I the LORD will make myself known unto him in a vision, and will speak unto him in a dream" (Num. 12:6).

"And it shall come to pass in the last days," saith God, "I will pour out of my Spirit upon all flesh: and your sons and your daughters shall prophesy, and your young men shall see visions, and your old men shall dream dreams" (Acts 2:17).

2. Asks God for dreams in faith. The Bible says we have not because we ask not (Jas. 4:2). So the Christian falls asleep at night asking God to speak to him through a dream.

3. Seeks God's interpretation of dreams he receives.

Then Daniel went in, and desired of the king that he would give him time, and that he would show the king the interpretation. Then Daniel went to his house, and made the thing known to Hananiah, Mishael, and Azariah, his companions: That they would desire mercies of the God of heaven concerning this secret; that Daniel and his fellows should not perish with the rest of the wise men of Babylon (Dan. 2:16-18).

4. Receives God's wisdom through dreams.

But there is a God in heaven that revealeth secrets, and maketh known to the king Nebuchadnezzar what shall be in the latter days. Thy dream, and the visions of thy head upon thy bed, are these (Dan 2:28).

5. Receives God's direction and faith through dreams.

But while he thought on these things, behold, the angel of the Lord appeared unto him in a dream, saying "Joseph, thou son of David, fear not to take unto thee Mary thy wife; for that which is conceived in her is of the Holy Ghost" (Matt. 1:20).

*And when they were departed, behold, the angel of
the Lord appeareth to Joseph in a dream, saying,
"Arise, and take the young child and his mother, and
flee into Egypt, and be thou there until I bring thee
word: for Herod will seek the young child to destroy
him" (Matt. 2:13).*

6. Acts in faith upon his dreams.

*When he arose, he took the young child and his mother
by night, and departed into Egypt (Matt. 2:14).*

7. Worships God for the dreams He gives.

*Then was the secret revealed unto Daniel in a night
vision. Then Daniel blessed the God of heaven. Daniel
answered and said, "Blessed be the name of God forever and ever: for wisdom and might are his" (Dan.
2:19,20).*

The New Age Movement and Dreams

1. Believes dreams come from the heart and spirit world.
Dreams may come either from your own heart or from the spiritual world. Since God rains on the just as well as the unjust,
some of the New Ager's dreams may be coming from God (Matt.
5:45). Others may be coming from other spiritual forces.

2. Seeks dreams. Is open and responsive to the world of dreams.

3. Seeks to interpret own dreams or seeks the help of others.
Explores the meaning of the dream, reads books on principles
for interpreting dreams, receives guidance on interpreting dreams.

4. Receives limited insight through dreams. As dreams do con-
tain messages, anyone who learns how to hear and understand
these messages will receive some insight.

5. Receives some direction and faith through dreams. Since
dreams can provide direction, he may receive direction from his
dreams.

6. May act upon dreams. Because he takes dreams seriously, he
is likely to act on his dreams.

7. Is thankful for what dreams teach. He is glad for the ability to receive wisdom through this means.

Phariseeism and Dreams

1. Generally views dreams as leftover, undigested food. The belief is that eating just before going to sleep causes dreams. Therefore, dreams are leftover, undigested food, and nothing to be taken seriously. Pharisees tend to believe in the false god of rationalism, which is "reliance upon reason to establish religious truth" (*Webster's*). Rationalism has no place for non-rational experiences such as dreams, visions or imagination. So all dreams, visions, and imagination found in Scripture are simply dismissed as something a Christian does not experience in this day and age. However, the Pharisee believes that New Agers and other "deceived" people could easily get caught up in such things. But not a Christian, for the Christian must go with rationalism. How is that for the traditions of men invalidating the Word of God, and then going one step further, to say that anyone who practices these sections of the Word of God is probably demonic, New Age or deceived? Kind of makes your head reel, doesn't it?

2. Doesn't ask God for dreams (therefore forgets most of them). Since dreams are not to be taken seriously, God would not be asked for a dream.

3. Doesn't seek any interpretation of dreams. Neither seeks nor needs God's interpretation of dreams, because time is not taken to receive or record dreams.

4. Doesn't receive any wisdom through dreams. This channel of God speaking is cut off.

5. Doesn't receive any direction or faith through dreams. This avenue of receiving instruction and faith from God is cut off.

6. Doesn't act in faith upon his dreams. No dream, no faith, and no faith-filled action.

7. Doesn't worship God for the gift of dreams. Despises dreams as a non-rational experience. Only rationalism is honored in his system for knowing.

51

Summary: Don't forget that counterfeits will do some of the same things that Christians do. That is what makes them good counterfeits. So don't let it bother you if the New Age is taking some of the same steps that a Christian takes when it comes to dreams.

Most New Agers believe in gravity, as do most Christians. Now, a Pharisee might have a fit about this. They might say, "See, New Agers believe in gravity, and the word `gravity' is never even mentioned in the Bible, and this doctrine is now seeping into the Church and some Christians are even using this non-biblical word `gravity' and getting other Christians involved in this deception!"

This is exactly the kind of thinking you will experience in religion. I have been told I should not use the words "center down," "incubation," "inner eye," etc. because New Agers use them and they are not in the Bible. Well, the experiences are in the Bible! You are to quiet yourself down, you are to mull over in your heart the things God is revealing to you, you are to use the eyes of your heart to see dream and vision.... Generally, I do try not to use "trigger" words which make people so nervous and fearful, but it surely is possible for a Christian to believe these things and use these words and not be a New Ager.

However, wouldn't it be nice if we grew up enough that we could actually have a vocabulary outside of Bible words and not be considered demonic or New Age in doing so? Nowhere in the Bible does it say that we cannot use words that are not used in the Bible. Nowhere in the Bible does it say that if an evil person uses a word, then a Christian should not. The whole thing becomes so ridiculous that the world just laughs in derision at the Church as we devour one another. No wonder they think we need government intervention to step in and monitor spiritual things. Otherwise Christians would just kill each other off.

The thing to remember is that counterfeits do NOT do some things that Christians do. That is what makes them counterfeits. In the case of the subject of this chapter, the New Age follower will NOT ask the Holy Spirit to interpret dreams. Nor will dreams be compared to the Bible to make sure that nothing the dreams lead him to do violate any biblical principle. That is where the New Ager goes wrong. It is not in seeking dreams and seeking to interpret dreams. No, that is fine. It is in not bringing these dreams back to the Holy Spirit and the Bible for interpretation and confirmation.

A GOOD COUNTERFEIT WILL BE VERY SIMILAR TO THE ORIGINAL! THAT IS OKAY. THAT IS TO BE EXPECTED. WHAT BETTER WAY IS THERE?

8

VISIONS

Vision defined: A flow of pictures generally seen on the screen inside one's mind, although they can be seen externally, as well. Visions can come from God or satan. If pictures come from self, I would place them in the category of a vain imagination. Imagination will be discussed in the next chapter.

In a vision, God can show pictures as plain "photographs," pictures shown as metaphors, and pictures shown as similes. They are all pictures and pictures move the heart. Ideas move the mind. Faith in the heart is generated through the use of pictures. Faith in the mind is generated through ideas. It is heart faith that moves mountains.

Christianity and Visions

1. Believes God grants visions today.
2. Asks God for visions in faith.
3. Looks for visions.
4. Receives God's perspective through visions.
5. Receives God's faith through visions.
6. Acts in faith upon God's visions.
7. Worships God for the visions He gives.

The New Age Movement and Visions

1. Believes visions come from the spiritual world.
2. Quiets to receive visions.
3. Looks for visions.
4. Receives visions from various spirit sources.
5. Receives some faith through his visions.
6. Acts in faith upon visions.
7. Is thankful for the experiences.

Phariseeism and Visions

1. Believes visions are not for today.
2. Does not ask God for visions.
3. Does not look for visions.
4. Sees negative pictures.
5. Receives satan's fear from demonic visions.
6. Acts in fear, and runs and hides.
7. Prays to escape this evil world.

Christianity and Visions

1. Believes God grants visions today.

And he said, "Hear now my words: If there be a prophet among you, I the LORD will make myself known unto him in a vision, and will speak unto him in a dream" (Num. 12:6).

"And it shall come to pass in the last days," saith God, "I will pour out of my Spirit upon all flesh: and your sons and your daughters shall prophesy, and your young men shall see visions, and your old men shall dream dreams" (Acts 2:17).

2. Asks God for visions in faith.
The Bible says we have not because we ask not (Jas. 4:2). So the Christian consciously asks God to give him a vision, particularly when in prayer.

3. Looks for visions.

I will stand upon my watch, and set me upon the tower, and will watch to see what he will say unto me, and what I shall answer when I am reproved. And the LORD answered me, and said, "Write the vision, and make it plain upon tables, that he may run that readeth it" (Hab. 2:1,2).

4. Receives God's perspective through visions. (Habakkuk 1-3)

The Lord replied, "Look at the nations and be amazed! For I am doing something in your own day, something you wouldn't believe even if someone told you about it. I am raising up the Babylonians to be a new power on the world scene. They are a cruel and violent nation who will march across the world and conquer it" (Hab. 1:5,6 NLT).

5. Receives God's faith through visions.

After these things the word of the LORD came unto Abram in a vision, saying, "Fear not, Abram: I am thy shield, and thy exceeding great reward...." And He brought him forth abroad, and said, "Look now toward heaven, and tell the stars, if thou be able to num-

ber them:" and He said unto him, "So shall thy seed be." And he believed in the LORD; and He counted it to him for righteousness (Gen. 15:1,5,6).

6. Acts in faith upon God's visions. In Acts 10, Peter was given a vision of unclean animals being lowered from heaven on a sheet, and was told to eat them. The Holy Spirit showed him through this vision that he was to receive the Gentiles into the Church, so the following day Peter arose and went to the house of Cornelius, a Gentile, and preached the gospel to him and his household. Peter acted in faith upon the vision he received.

7. Worships God for the visions He gives.

Although the fig tree shall not blossom, neither shall fruit be in the vines; the labour of the olive shall fail, and the fields shall yield no meat; the flock shall be cut off from the fold, and there shall be no herd in the stalls: Yet I will rejoice in the LORD, I will joy in the God of my salvation. The LORD God is my strength, and he will make my feet like hinds' feet, and he will make me to walk upon mine high places. To the chief singer on my stringed instruments (Hab. 3:17-19).

The New Age Movement and Visions

1. Believes visions come from the spiritual world. Believes there is a spirit world and that visions are a way of interacting with this world.

2. Quiets to receive visions. Centers down to receive these visions.

3. Looks for visions. Is trained to look for vision.

4. Receives visions from various spirit sources. Receives visions from evil spirits and from the Holy Spirit. Since he is not going through Jesus Christ, he will receive demonic visions, and satan coming to him as an angel of light (II Cor. 11:14). Because God rains on the just as well as the unjust, even a New Ager may receive visions from God (Matt. 5:45). A biblical example is Balaam the "false" prophet receiving a true vision from God (Num. 22:8-12; II Pet. 2:15).

5. Receives some faith through the visions. An increased level of faith is a by-product of gazing upon a vision. This may be faith toward moving in the right direction or faith toward moving in the wrong direction, depending on whether the vision came from God or from satan.

6. Acts in faith upon the visions. Since New Agers believe in vision, and look for vision, they will also act upon the visions they receive.

7. Is thankful for the experiences. He is thankful for the visions he receives.

Phariseeism and Visions

1. Believes visions are not for today. Believes that since the Bible has come, we no longer need visions (I Cor. 13:10).

2. Does not ask God for visions. Since there is not faith that visions are for today, they are not asked for.

3. Does not look for visions. Believes visions are a thing of the past and does not look for them.

4. Sees negative pictures. Through the sin of omission (of not presenting the eyes of his heart to God to fill), satan's pictures flood his visionary capacity (Jas. 4:17). You see, there are no spiritual vacuums in the universe. Satan quickly fills whatever is not purposely presented to God. Thus, generally the Pharisee has many negative demonic pictures filling his mind.

5. Receives satan's fear from demonic visions. The visions will probably be of the takeover of the world by satan and his cohorts (i.e., the antichrist and evil men). And since emotions are by-products of pictures, the Pharisee will most likely live in fear, doubt and pessimism.

6. Acts in fear, and runs and hides. Acts on the visions held before his eyes. Purchases places in the hills where he prepares for a one-world government ruled by the antichrist.

7. Prays to escape this evil world. Rather than thanksgiving, there is a passionate desire to be taken out of this evil world.

Summary: There is no excuse for the Pharisee not yielding the eyes of his heart to the Lord Jesus Christ and asking Him to fill them with dream and vision. If you have not done so, I encourage you to repent today, and present yourself now as a living sacrifice to God to fill and flow through (Rom. 12:1,2).

If you are a New Ager, it is dangerous to go into the spiritual world without being a born-again Christian, and entering in the name of the Lord Jesus Christ. Satan comes as an angel of light seeking whom he may devour (II Cor. 11:14, I Pet. 5:8). He is real. He is alive, and he does destroy people's lives. However, there is no need to be devoured by satan. Repent and give your life to the Lord Jesus Christ and then you can enter the world of dream and vision and imagination safely. See Appendix A to learn how to be born again.

9

IMAGINATION

Imagination defined: "Forming a mental image" (***Webster's***).

My definition: "Thinking with pictures" (right-brain thinking) as opposed to analytical structured thoughts (left-brain thinking). Imagination is used to give us metaphors and similes.

Picturing is different from vision in that visions are a flow of pictures not being controlled by you. Your picturing, your imagination, is controlled by you.

Christianity and Imagination

1. Believes God created the imagination.

2. Believes the imaginative capacity is to be yielded to God to be filled in the ways He wants it filled.

3. Hides Scripture in his imagination.

4. Uses imagination when he reasons.

5. Uses imagination when he prays.

6. Uses imagination when he meditates on Scripture.

7. Thanks God for the gift of imagination.

The New Age Movement and Imagination (Visualization)

1. Believes imagination is the result of evolution.

2. Believes he should use his imagination himself.

3. Uses imagination to improve self-esteem.

4. Uses imagination to improve creativity.

5. Uses imagination to construct a positive worldview.

6. Uses imagination when he meditates.

7. Is thankful for the ability to imagine.

Phariseeism and Imagination

1. Believes all imagination is vain imagination.

2. Ignores and does not use his imaginative capacity.

3. Is filled with demonic imaginations.

4. Uses positive imaginations to enhance the power of satan.

5. Uses negative imaginations when viewing the Church's power.

6. Uses negative imaginations when interpreting Scripture.

7. Lives in fear because of negative imaginations.

Christianity and Imagination

1. Believes God created the imagination. Since God created man in his totality, God created man's ability to imagine.

> *So God created man in his own image, in the image of God created he him; male and female created he them (Gen. 1:27).*

2. Believes the imaginative capacity is to be yielded to God to be filled in the ways He wants it filled. Just like every other part of our beings, we are to present our imaginative abilities before God to fill and flow through.

> *I beseech you therefore, brethren, by the mercies of God, that ye present your bodies a living sacrifice, holy, acceptable unto God, which is your reasonable service (Rom. 12:1).*

3. Hides Scripture in the imagination. When reading the Bible, pictures and imagines the scenes. They are hidden in the imagination of the heart.

> *O LORD God of Abraham, Isaac, and of Israel, our fathers, keep this for ever in the imagination of the thoughts of the heart of thy people, and prepare their heart unto thee (I Chron. 29:18).*

4. Uses imagination when reasoning. Rather than limiting reason to analysis only (a left-hemisphere brain function), makes it a whole-brain function and reasons using pictures as well as thoughts. Notice how God asks us to reason.

> *"Come now, and let us reason together," saith the LORD: "though your sins be as scarlet, they shall be as white as snow; though they be red like crimson, they shall be as wool" (Is. 1:18).*

5. Uses imagination when praying.

> *The LORD is my shepherd; I shall not want. He maketh me to lie down in green pastures: he leadeth me beside the still waters. He restoreth my soul: he leadeth me in the paths of righteousness for his name's sake.*

Yea, though I walk through the valley of the shadow of death, I will fear no evil: for thou art with me; thy rod and thy staff they comfort me. Thou preparest a table before me in the presence of mine enemies: thou anointest my head with oil; my cup runneth over. Surely goodness and mercy shall follow me all the days of my life: and I will dwell in the house of the LORD forever (Ps. 23).

6. Uses imagination when meditating on Scripture.

This book of the law shall not depart out of thy mouth; but thou shalt meditate therein day and night, that thou mayest observe to do according to all that is written therein: for then thou shalt make thy way prosperous, and then thou shalt have good success (Josh. 1:8).

The word "meditate" in the above verse has as part of its root, literal meaning the word "image." (See #1897 in **Strong's Concordance** and also the Hebrew dictionary at the end of **Strong's Concordance**.) So part of meditating on the Bible is to imagine it. Thus, imagination is not evil. It is to be filled with biblical pictures, and presented to God to fill with His dream and vision.

7. Thanks God for the gift of imagination. The Christian gives thanks to God for all things. That includes his imagination.

Giving thanks always for all things unto God and the Father in the name of our Lord Jesus Christ (Eph. 5:20).

The New Age Movement and Imagination (Visualization)

1. Believes imagination is the result of evolution. Man evolved and was not created by a Creator.

2. Believes in using the imagination. Man is to maximize the use of all his faculties and talents.

3. Uses imagination to improve self-esteem. By picturing positive things about self, man can improve his self-esteem.

4. Uses imagination to improve creativity. Imagination is a link to creative ideas. So imagination is used extensively in creativity sessions.

5. Uses imagination to construct a positive worldview. Believes that if you will picture a positive world, you can help create a positive world.

6. Uses imagination when meditating. Whole-brain thinking is taught and practiced as part of meditation.

7. Is thankful for ability to imagine. Glad for this capacity and ability as is glad for all capacities and abilities possessed.

Phariseeism and Imagination

1. Believes all imagination is vain imagination.
Because that, when they knew God, they glorified Him not as God, neither were thankful; but became vain in their imaginations, and their foolish heart was darkened (Rom. 1:21).

2. Ignores and does not use imaginative capacity. Believes imagination and visualization have shaman or New Age roots, so refuse to use them in a positive sense.

3. Is filled with demonic imaginations. Whatever is not purposely presented to God is quickly filled with satan.

4. Uses positive imaginations to enhance the power of satan. Believes the antichrist is strong and powerful, and will chase the Church around and persecute Her.

5. Uses negative imaginations when viewing the Church's power. Pictures the Church as weak and at the mercy of the antichrist.

6. Uses negative imaginations when interpreting Scripture. Satan helps imagine the worst-case scenario when interpreting or visualizing the fulfillment of Bible prophecies.

7. Lives in fear because of negative imaginations. Negative pictures produce negative emotions such as fear.

Summary: That which is not purposely presented to God is quickly filled by satan. Since Pharisees do not purposely present their imaginative abilities to God, satan fills them and they have horrible pictures of the power of the antichrist devouring the Church. Of course, every Pharisee can back up his position with Scripture. The Pharisees of Jesus' day surely could. Even satan in the desert could back up his temptations of Jesus with Scripture (e.g., Matt. 4:5,6). So just because someone has a Scripture verse which he thinks supports his position doesn't at all prove that his position is right. Perhaps he is using the wrong Scripture verse. Perhaps he is misapplying it. The one thing I know is that the Church was commissioned and empowered to disciple all nations. That surely is what should fill the Christian's imagination, not some takeover of the planet by satan.

10

SELF-ESTEEM/POSITIVE IMAGING

Christianity and Self-Esteem/Positive Imaging

1. Believes man is a vessel designed to be filled with God.

2. Believes when Jesus is invited into life, the Holy Spirit becomes joined to the spirit.

3. Seeks to live tuned to the Spirit, believing as this is done, man becomes an expression of Christ.

4. Seeks to do nothing on own initiative but instead live out of the Holy Spirit within.

5. Believes they can do all things through Christ Who strengthens them.

6. Has extremely high self-esteem, because they live conscious of the "Christ I" rather than the "self I."

7. Worships God for the great mystery that has been revealed, of Christ within, which transforms current and future life.

The New Age Movement and Self-Esteem/Positive Imaging

1. Believes man is created to live connected to the spiritual forces of the universe.

2. Believes when connected to the universal energy, life is enhanced.

3. Seeks to live tuned to the universal energy source.

4. Seeks to stay centered, and not do things on own accord.

5. Believes the universal energy allows unlimited opportunity.

6. Has a bright self-esteem because of his connection to the universal energy field.

7. Is thankful for discovering the universal energy field.

(Note: Since Jesus is the underlying force in the universe Who holds all things together - Colossians 1:17 - it is possible for non-Christians to tap God's energy *to a certain level.*)

Phariseeism and Self-Esteem/Positive Imaging

1. Believes man is a self-contained unit who is able to think, speak, and act alone.

2. Has no revelation that Christ is joined to them.

3. Has little consciousness of Holy Spirit flow in life.

4. Have done most things on their own initiative.

5. Doesn't have a revelation of Philippians 4:13.

6. Has a low self-esteem and sees self as a worm.

7. Thanks God that as a miserable sinner, God still has chosen to give eternal life.

Christianity and Self-Esteem/Positive Imaging

1. Believes man is a vessel designed to be filled with God.

But we have this treasure in earthen vessels, that the excellency of the power may be of God, and not of us (II Cor. 4:7).

Man is not a self-contained unit, able to think, act and speak on his own. Man is hollow. He is a vessel. He is designed to be filled by another and to have another flow out through him. That other is to be Almighty God, and we are to express Him to the world.

2. Believes when Jesus is invited into life, the Holy Spirit becomes joined to the spirit.

But he that is joined unto the Lord is one spirit (I Cor. 6:17).

Whereby are given unto us exceeding great and precious promises: that by these ye might be partakers of the divine nature (II Pet. 1:4).

As Christians, our spirits are joined to the Holy Spirit, and we have received the divine nature of God within us. Therefore, at the core of our beings we are now joined to Almighty God. When we look inward, we see God.

3. Seeks to live tuned to the Spirit ("flow"- Jn. 7:37-39), believing that as he does, he becomes an expression of Christ (Gal. 5:25).

Jesus stood and cried, saying, "If any man thirst, let him come unto me, and drink. He that believeth on me, as the scripture hath said, out of his belly shall flow rivers of living water." But this spake he of the Spirit, which they that believe on him should receive: for the Holy Ghost was not yet given; because that Jesus was not yet glorified (Jn. 7:37-39).

If we live in the Spirit, let us also walk in the Spirit (Gal. 5:25).

Since we know we are hollow and the Holy Spirit lives within us, we now tune to the flow of the Holy Spirit within. As we live out of this flow, we become expressions of Christ living, rather than simply us living. Western rationalism teaches instead that man should live out of the reasoning of his mind.

4. Seeks to do nothing on his own initiative but instead live out of the Holy Spirit within.

Then answered Jesus and said unto them, "Verily, verily, I say unto you, The Son can do nothing of himself, but what he seeth the Father do: for what things soever he doeth, these also doeth the Son likewise. For the Father loveth the Son, and showeth him all things that himself doeth: and he will show him greater works than these, that ye may marvel (Jn. 5:19,20).

I can of mine own self do nothing: as I hear, I judge: and my judgment is just; because I seek not mine own will, but the will of the Father which hath sent me (Jn. 5:30).

The Christian does not live out of his own reason or his own abilities or his own strength. Rather, he lives out of the Father's initiative, which is sensed as a "flow." Therefore, the Christian is constantly tuned to flow as he walks through life.

5. Believes he can do all things through Christ Who strengthens him.

I can do all things through Christ which strengtheneth me (Phil. 4:13).

The Christian who is tuned to the flow of the Holy Spirit within discovers an unlimited power of God flowing out through him. This anoints him to do exceedingly above what he is normally capable of doing.

6. Has extremely high self-esteem, because he lives conscious of the "Christ I" rather than the "self I.".

I am crucified with Christ: nevertheless I live; yet not I, but Christ liveth in me: and the life which I now live in the flesh I live by the faith of the Son of God, who loved me, and gave himself for me (Gal. 2:20).

God has given the Christian a spiritual revelation of this verse. Christians see that, indeed, what is flowing out of them is God and not themselves. Christians are conscious of the river within them rather than being conscious of their own limited thoughts, ideas and strength.

7. Worships God for the great mystery that has been revealed, of Christ within, which transforms current and future life.
To whom God would make known what is the riches of the glory of this mystery among the Gentiles; which is Christ in you, the hope of glory (Col 1:27).

Christians live in constant worship to Almighty God because He has granted the riches of being able to house the God of the universe within his temple of dust. Truly, we are dust fused to Glory!

The New Age Movement and Self-Esteem/Positive Imaging

1. Believes man is created to live connected to the spiritual forces of the universe. There is a spiritual energy permeating the entire universe to which man can connect. This pulse of life is in everything. This lines up with Colossians 1:17, "And He is before all things, and by Him all things consist." Christ surely is the power and energy holding every atom together. New Agers know there is a power flowing out from every molecule; they just don't know it is the power of the Lord Jesus Christ.

2. Believes when connected to the universal energy, life is enhanced. When connected to this energy source, life is enhanced. A power beyond self is drawn upon.

3. Seeks to live tuned to the universal energy source. Seeks to connect with this energy source through numerous strategies, one being centering down and touching the spirit.

4. Seeks to stay centered, and not do things on own accord. Believes in allowing this energy to flow out through the body, rather than just do things on own accord.

5. Believes the universal energy allows unlimited opportunity. Understands that when connected to this energy field many extraordinary activities can be preformed.

6. Has a bright self-esteem because of a connection to the universal energy field. Sees self as living connected to the power of god and feels confident to overcome.

7. Is thankful for discovering the universal energy field. Glad to have experienced this power which fills the universe and is eager to share it with others.

Phariseeism and Self-Esteem/Positive Imaging

1. Believes man is a self-contained unit who is able to think, speak, and act on his own. A typical refrain is, "God gave you a brain and you're supposed to use it." A key idea is that we are to try, to strive, to fight the good fight, to be diligent, to serve, to love. The emphasis is on doing these things ourselves.

2. Has no revelation that Christ is joined to him. Looks within and sees self, not Christ. Has no revelation of being dead to personal effort, and is to draw upon the power of Christ within.

3. Has little consciousness of Holy Spirit flowing in life. The concept of "flow" has not registered. Thinks in terms of the use of reason and self-effort.

4. Does most things out of his own initiative (e.g., because he decides to do them, or assumes it would be a good thing God would want him to do). The idea that "I do nothing on my own initiative" is a foreign concept to him. Essentially, everything he does is on his own initiative. He thinks it up and he does it.

5. Doesn't have a revelation of Philippians 4:13 and what the Holy Spirit can release through him. He is great at quoting Scriptures, but generally does not have a revelation of what the verses really mean as they are worked out in his life.

6. Has low self-esteem and sees himself as a worm. It is called "worm theology," and can be supported by scripture. "Fear not, thou worm Jacob" (Is. 41:14). Tends to see self as the underdog, as the one who is downtrodden.

7. **Thanks God that as a miserable sinner God still has chosen to give eternal life.** Generally conscious of sinfulness and weakness, the Pharisee is grateful that God has offered to save him, despite his sinful condition.

Summary: Man alone is too small a package to have a valid positive self-esteem. Man joined to Almighty God and living out of Him has every right to have a healthy self-esteem, because God is living His life out through him.

You don't need self-help tapes to tell that you are great. You need to tune to God's voice and let Him tell you about His love for you and what He is preparing to do through you.

If you can't hear God's voice, or don't believe He is talking anymore today, then you probably suffer from poor self-esteem. Your solution: Discover God's voice within your heart and let Him speak to you daily.

11

THANKSGIVING AND A POSITIVE MENTAL ATTITUDE

Christianity and Praise & Worship

1. Believes God rules.

2. Gives thanks in everything.

3. Gives thanks for everything.

4. Expects all things to work together for good.

The New Age Movement and a Positive Mental Attitude

1. Believes fate rules.

2. Maintains a positive attitude in every situation.

3. Finds the good in every situation.

4. Expects all things to work out for the best.

Phariseeism and a Negative Mental Attitude

1. Believes satan, the prince of the power of the air, rules.

2. Grumbles and complains in most situations.

3. Finds fault with everything that is new or different.

4. Expects all things to be manipulated by satan toward evil.

Christianity and Praise & Worship

1. Believes God rules

The most High ruleth in the kingdom of men, and giveth it to whomsoever he will (Dan. 4:25).

God has always believed that He rules this universe. That includes the earth, the realm of mankind. The Christian believes this. He also believes God rules in the realm of mankind, which sets the stage for him to be filled with praise and worship.

2. Gives thanks in everything.

In every thing give thanks: for this is the will of God in Christ Jesus concerning you (I Thess. 5:18).

The Bible is clear that no matter what the situation, you simply give thanks. Thus, Christians are extremely positive and grateful people.

3. Gives thanks for everything.

Giving thanks always for all things unto God and the Father in the name of our Lord Jesus Christ (Eph. 5:20).

Not only do Christian give thanks *in* every situation, they give thanks *for* every situation. Because God rules and works all things after the counsel of His will, the Christian can thank God for all things (Eph. 1:11).

4. Expects all things to work together for good.

And we know that all things work together for good to them that love God, to them who are the called according to his purpose (Rom. 8:28).

Regardless of how negative a situation first appears, by maintaining a thankful heart, filled with praise and worship, God has promised that He will work it out for your good. This surely happened as Paul and Silas sang hymns of praise to God while in the stocks of a prison and God sent an earthquake to set them free (Acts 16:22-29).

The New Age Movement and a Positive Mental Attitude

1. Believes fate rules. There is no personal god in this universe, so things just happen. Fate rules your life.

2. Maintains a positive attitude in every situation. By staying positive, positive energy is drawn to the New Ager. Negativity draws negative energy. Therefore, staying positive is the key to the best life has to offer.

3. Finds the good in every situation. Part of staying positive is looking to see what can be learned in each and every situation, learning it, and going on to new heights.

4. Expects all things to work out for the best. By pressing on and working together with "the force," life will get better and better.

Phariseeism and a Negative Mental Attitude

1. Believes satan, the prince of the power of the air, rules.
Wherein in time past ye walked according to the course of this world, according to the prince of the power of the air, the spirit that now worketh in the children of disobedience (Eph. 2:2).

Starts with the belief that satan rules this planet and thus situations are going to get worse and worse.

2. Grumbles and complains in most situations.
How long shall I bear with this evil congregation, which murmur against me? I have heard the murmurings of the children of Israel, which they murmur against me. Say unto them, As truly as I live, saith the LORD, as ye have spoken in mine ears, so will I do to you (Num. 14:27,28).

Tends to grumble and complain about almost everything, every day, all the time. Becomes extremely negative.

3. Finds fault with everything that is new or different.

*Behold, I will do a new thing; now it shall spring forth
(Is. 43:19).*

Always wishes life could go back to the way it was in yester-
year. That was a better time. Hates change. Resists change. Has
no consciousness of God doing new things. New things are called
"Christian fads" or, worse yet, "New Age deceptions."

4. Expects all things to be manipulated by satan toward evil.

Completely convinced that satan will get himself into everything, including government, entertainment, business, money, and
education, and make them worse and worse. Prophesies gloom
and doom over all these institutions. Expects the worst and gets
the worst.

Summary: I grew up a Pharisee. Why would anyone want such a
negative lifestyle? Well, I was at one point in my life convinced
biblically that this was the only lifestyle available to mankind, so
I took it. Now I see differently. I see the risen Christ, not the
antichrist. I see the power of God, not the power of satan. I speak
the power of God, not the power of satan. And I act in faith on
the power of God, not the power of satan. Try it. You'll like it! It
sure beats believing for the takeover of the planet by satan.

New Agers, there is a personal loving God Who rules the universe and wants to fill your heart and mind. Give yourself to Him
by accepting Jesus Christ as your Lord and Savior, and you shall
be saved. See Appendix A.

12

JOURNALING VERSUS AUTOMATIC WRITING

Christianity and Journaling

1. Believes journaling is like the writing of the prophets, in which prayers and what God speaks back are both written down.

2. Believes journaling can be a part of daily devotional time.

3. Believes writing prayers is a way of releasing the flow of the Holy Spirit within.

The New Age Movement and Automatic Writing

1. Believes automatic writing is a way of receiving words from the "evocative other."

2. Believes automatic writing can be a regular activity whenever connection to the spirit world is sought.

3. Believes automatic writing can be a way of clearly receiving from the spirit world.

Phariseeism and Journaling

1. Believes journaling would be adding to Scripture.

2. Believes journaling should not be a part of your devotional time.

3. Believes the release of the flow of the Holy Spirit in your life should not be sought.

Christianity and Journaling

1. Believes journaling is like the writing of the prophets, in which prayers and what God speaks back are written down.
And the LORD answered me, and said, "Write the vi-sion, and make it plain upon tables, that he may run that readeth it" (Hab. 2:2).

The book of Psalms is an example of the writing of one's two-way dialogue with Almighty God, as are the prophets, as well as the whole book of Revelation. Hundreds of chapters of Scripture demonstrate the process of journaling.

2. Believes journaling can be a part of daily devotional time.
It surely appears that King David made journaling a part of his daily devotional life. Many Christians have made journaling a regular part of their daily devotional lives, discovering great benefit from it.

3. Believes writing prayers is a way of releasing the flow of the Holy Spirit within. Journaling allows the believer to stay in faith for five, ten, fifteen minutes or more, and simply write what is sensed as coming from God. As you fix your eyes on Jesus, tune to "flow" (i.e., the Holy Spirit within) and simply write in faith, you will receive page after page of dialogue with Almighty God. By journaling, you have the freedom to test the flow after it has been written down. Since it can be tested later, the Christian can stay in faith as it is received, thus staying in faith for a longer period of time and receiving more from God. Those who come to God must come in faith, not doubt (Heb. 11:6). Journaling helps the Christian come in faith and stay in faith for extended periods of time, knowing it can be tested later.

The New Age Movement and Automatic Writing

1. Believes automatic writing is a way of receiving words from the "evocative other." Automatic writing is a way for a New Ager to receive from the spirit realm. Key differences between this experience and the biblical experience of journaling exist. In automatic writing, the person's hand hangs limp and a spirit takes control of the hand and writes, while in journaling, the

Christian has his eyes fixed on Jesus, is tuned to flow from within his heart, and chooses to write that which is flowing within. Thus, in automatic writing, only the hand is involved. In journaling, the heart and flow from within are also involved.

2. Believes automatic writing can be a regular activity whenever you seek to connect to the spirit world. New Agers will use automatic writing daily as a way to connect with the spirit world. Books of this kind of dialogue with the spirit world can be purchased in secular bookstores. I do not recommend that you purchase these books. They have deception in them.

3. Believes automatic writing can be a way of clearly receiving from the spirit world. New Agers do receive clear messages from the spirit world through automatic writing. However, since they are not going through the Lord Jesus Christ, they are receiving impressions from many spirits, including evil spirits and perhaps even satan. So the message may be clear, but the source will often be defiled, and thus the message will be defiled.

Phariseeism and Journaling

1. Believes journaling would be adding to Scripture.
> *For I testify unto every man that heareth the words of the prophecy of this book, If any man shall add unto these things, God shall add unto him the plagues that are written in this book (Rev. 22:18).*

Therefore, if anyone were to write down anything he received from God, it would be viewed as trying to be equivalent to Scripture and thus adding to Scripture and he would be cursed with plagues.

However, this line of reasoning is faulty, because all journaling does not become Scripture. Even David mentions some journaling God gave him (concerning the design of the Temple) which did not become Scripture (I Chron. 28:19).

2. Believes journaling should not be a part of your devotional time. Obviously if journaling is adding to Scripture, it should not be done.

84

3. Believes the release of the flow of the Holy Spirit should not be sought. Holy Spirit flow is not an idea that religion has any comprehension of. Religion is of the flesh and persecutes those who are of the Spirit (Gal. 4:21-31).

Summary: Journaling is different from automatic writing. Automatic writing is the counterfeit to journaling. Spiritual people journal to catch the words of the Holy Spirit. Religious people do not journal because they do not believe God is speaking anymore today.

13

YOUR EPISTEMOLOGY: HOW DO YOU KNOW?

Although the following information is set up in a chart form of six points each, the points do not correspond across the chart from the Christian to the New Ager to the Pharisee. That is because their approaches are so different there is no easy correlation. Therefore, as you read the chart below you will discover three totally different methodologies for discovering truth.

Your epistemology is your system for knowing. Decide what system for knowing you use. When I was younger I never reflected upon my epistemology, and I have actually used several different approaches to knowing throughout my life. For the last twenty years, I have used the epistemology described below for Christianity. If you are not using the system for knowing that is taught in the Bible, then I suggest you change and begin using it.

How Does a Christian Know?

1. God illumines Scripture to your heart and mind.

2. God anoints your reasoning.

3. God grants peace or unrest in your heart.

4. God speaks to you through the anointed counsel of others.

5. God grants an illumined understanding of life's experiences.

6. God grants revelation through dream, vision and prophecy.

How Does a New Ager Know?

1. Explores and reads widely.

2. Asks, "What am I receiving from the spiritual world?"

3. Asks, "What does my experience tell me?"

4. Asks, "What does the experience of others, especially 'masters' in the area, teach me?"

5. Asks what can careful scientific exploration of the spirit world teach me?

6. Asks, "Where is the next step of our evolution taking us?"

How Does a Pharisee Know?

1. Heathens do it, so it must be bad.

2. It is Eastern, so it must be bad.

3. It involves spiritual encounter, so it must be bad.

4. It is new and different, so it must be bad.

5. I don't understand it, so it must be bad.

6. I am not sure about it, so I will call it evil.

How Does a Christian Know?

Pillar One - Illumined Scriptures

And they said one to another, "Did not our heart burn within us, while He talked with us by the way, and while He opened to us the scriptures" (Lk. 24:32)?

This pillar is experienced as the Holy Spirit illumines Scriptures to us - we sense them leaping off the page or just coming to our attention spontaneously. It is a result of meditating upon the Scriptures. See Appendix B for a seven-step approach to biblical meditation.

Pillar Two - Illumined Thoughts in Your Mind

Having carefully investigated all of these accounts from the beginning, I have decided to write a careful summary for you... (Lk. 1:3 NLT)

This pillar is experienced as the Holy Spirit guides our reasoning processes through spontaneous impressions. It is obvious that Luke's gospel was **more** than simply investigative research of his own mind, as what he wrote has stood as the Word of God for 2000 years. This is different from simple reasoning in that, when we reason, we are controlling the reasoning process. When we are having illumined thoughts, or anointed reasoning, we are allowing the flow of the Holy Spirit to guide the reasoning process.

Pillar Three - Illumined Witness in Your Heart

And immediately when Jesus perceived in His spirit that they so reasoned within themselves, He said unto them, "Why reason ye these things in your hearts?" (Mk. 2:8).

And let the peace of God rule in your hearts, to the which also ye are called in one body; and be ye thankful (Col. 3:15).

This pillar is experienced as immediate spiritual (intuitive) knowing and peace or unrest on the spirit level. Mothers often know immediately when their children are in danger and need prayer or help. Words of wisdom and words of knowledge come this way. It is different from peace or unrest on the soul level in that it is deeper - it is in our innermost beings. It takes a bit of skill to learn to differentiate between these two levels of peace and unrest.

Pillar Four - Illumined Counsel of Others

Where no counsel is, the people fall: but in the multitude of counselors there is safety (Prov. 11:14).

This pillar is experienced when spiritual advisors are asked to seek God for confirmation, additions, or adjustments in the guidance we sense God has given. There are several distinctions between this kind of counsel and just any old counsel from anyone. First, one is going to spiritually mature men and women. Secondly, one is going to people who are ahead in the area of counsel being sought. Lastly, one does not ask for the counselor's best ideas on the topic; but asks for prayer about the issue and for them to tell what they sense God is saying to them about it. We do not want any of Sarah's un-anointed counsel (Gen. 16:1,2).

Pillar Five - Illumined Understanding of Life's Experiences

Ye shall know them by their fruits. Do men gather grapes of thorns, or figs of thistles? (Matt. 7:16).

This pillar is experienced as we ask God to give us insight and understanding concerning the fruit life is demonstrating. God gives us revelation as to what has caused the fruit.

For example, in Habakkuk 1-3 we find Habakkuk faced with a distressing situation as the Babylonians came to destroy Israel. When he prayed and journaled about it, God revealed to him the reason the destruction of Israel must come, and Habakkuk concluded in worship (Hab. 3:17-19). This is different from just observing situations with the natural eye and deciding on our own what truth is. This involves taking the situation to God in prayer and letting Him show us what He is doing in the midst of the situation, and what He wants our response to be.

Pillar Six - Illumined Revelation from God through Dreams, Visions, Prophecy, and Journaling

"And it shall come to pass in the last days," saith God, "I will pour out of my Spirit upon all flesh: and your

> *sons and your daughters shall prophesy, and your young men shall see visions, and your old men shall dream dreams" (Acts 2:17).*

This pillar is experienced as we receive direct revelation from God through dreams, visions, and prophecy.

The wise leader has a solid foundation of Scripture within him, which underlies the use of these six pillars and has a goal of glorifying God in all he does. He looks for all six of the pillars to line up before he assumes a direction.

How Does a New Ager Know?

1. Explores and reads widely. New Agers read and explore widely. They have little restrictions philosophically or theologically. They feel free to read from various disciplines and from various perspectives. They are not trying to defend a particular theology or philosophy. They believe the Bible is a good book and Jesus was a great mystic. However, to them the Bible is not inerrant, and Jesus Christ is not the Son of God and Savior of the world.

2. Asks, "What am I receiving from the spiritual world?" New Agers are open and seeking spiritual experiences. These experiences are valued highly and what they gain through them is an important element in leading them toward truth, as they understand it.

3. Asks, "What does my experience tell me?" They believe experience is a very good teacher. They will catalog their experiences to see what they can learn. Jung, for instance, cataloged 50,000 dreams in his lifetime.

4. Asks, "What does the experience of others, especially masters in the area, teach me?" They receive from others, and search out "masters" in the area they are studying, for mentoring. They will travel far and wide to sit under these masters and learn from them.

5. Asks, "What can careful scientific exploration of the spirit world teach me?" They are wide open to new scientific instruments for measuring spiritual phenomena. They experiment and train using these instruments. By bringing greater objectiveness to their spiritual experiences, they are able to quickly train others how to move into spiritual phenomena.

6. Asks, "Where is the next step of our evolution taking us?" They believe strongly that life is evolving, and there is a step of higher consciousness lying before us. They press in to discover what this next level is, and to experience it themselves.

How Does a Pharisee Know?

1. Heathens do it, so it must be bad. This is where they start their discovery of truth. They start by studying the counterfeit. If a heathen does it, then automatically Christians can't. This is so totally backward as an approach for discovering truth that it would be laughable, were it not so widely believed and practiced. Many books on the market today start and end with this backward premise.

One reason this is such a poor standard for discovering truth (aside from the fact that it is NEVER TAUGHT IN SCRIPTURES - AND IS THUS UNSCRIPTURAL) is that it actually violates Scriptural principles.

The Bible teaches that God rains on the just AND THE UN-JUST (Matt. 5:45), which means that God's truth can pour down even upon a non-Christian. Biblical examples of non-Christians having truth include Moses' father-in-law Jethro, a heathen, from whom Moses received wise counsel that he acted upon (Ex. 18). Daniel spent three years being trained in Nebuchadnezzar's court, learning the "literature and the language of the Chaldeans" (Dan. 1:4,5) and yet "God gave him knowledge and intelligence in every branch of literature and wisdom; Daniel even understood all kinds of visions and dreams" (Dan. 1:17). God can overlay your learning with an anointing of the Holy Spirit and help you see things others don't see. This will cause your superiors to be impressed with your knowledge and performance (Dan. 1:19).

2. It is Eastern, so it must be bad. This assumes that Western thought processes are good and right and biblical, and Eastern are not. This assumes that Jesus was a Westerner, and that people with Western mindsets wrote the Bible. This could not be further from the truth. Jesus was not a Westerner. Jesus was born and raised in the Middle East. Mostly people with a Hebrew mindset wrote the Bible, which is much closer to the eastern mindset than it is to the Western mindset.

Where in the Bible does it say that Western is good and Eastern is bad? Come on, folks. Let's use biblically stated standards for discovering truth, not ones we just pull out of our hats.

The way Westerners handle the Bible is not the way it is intended to be handled. It is a book full of stories of people's encounters with Almighty God. It is meant to encourage us to have our own encounters with Almighty God, not to replace them, as so many have allowed it to do.

3. It involves spiritual encounter, so it must be bad. This, too, would be laughable if it were not so widely taught and believed. Obviously, if the traditions of men (dispensationalism and demythalization) have removed all opportunity for a Christian to have his own spiritual encounters with God through dream, vision, hearing God's voice, experiencing God's power, and having His gifts flowing through them, then anyone who has such experiences must be evil.

So now, even though the Bible is full of Spirit-encounter from Genesis to Revelation, anyone today who does such things is declared to be a New Ager or an Eastern cultist of some kind.

4. It is new and different, so it must be bad. The belief here is that the way it was is the way it should be. These people always resist change, and drag along about 50 to 100 years behind the rest of the culture.

What we should realize is that the only constant is change. Nowhere does the Bible teach that new is necessarily evil. As a matter of fact, it teaches the opposite: "Behold, I will do a new thing; now it shall spring forth; shall ye not know it?" (Is. 43:19). Jesus even said to His disciples, "I have yet many things to say unto you, but ye cannot bear them now" (Jn. 16:12). So it is obvious that, if we keep progressing in the Spirit, Jesus has things to tell us which He didn't tell the disciples. That is totally unacceptable to a Pharisee.

5. I don't understand it, so it must be bad. Many immediately use this approach to discovering truth. They say, "This is new and different and confusing to me." Actually, all new things have the potential of shaking up our existing paradigms and thus causing some confusion as we must now discover a new paradigm, which embraces the new truth. So our minds will go through periods of confusion as they discover and integrate new things. Einstein's theory of relativity and his ideas on quantum physics totally changed science's paradigm of 500 years.

The Bible says that we are to "trust in the LORD with all thine heart; and **lean not unto thine own understanding.** In all thy ways acknowledge him, and he shall direct thy paths" (Prov. 3:5,6). Our walk depends not so much on our reasoned-out theology as it does our faith in God. Reason is only commanded in the Bible if we do it TOGETHER with God (Is. 1:18). Reasoning on our own (i.e., without illumination) is never encouraged in the Bible, even though the false god of rationalism requires it.

6. I am not sure about it, so I will call it evil. Some people feel the safest thing to do when they are not sure about something is to tell people that it is uncertain and appears suspect so it is best if they leave it alone so they don't get caught up in something that is wrong. The Bible says:

> *"Woe unto them that call evil good, and good evil;*
> *that put darkness for light, and light for darkness; that*
> *put bitter for sweet, and sweet for bitter!" (Is. 5:20)*

If something is good and right and you tell people to steer clear of it, you are on God's "woe list." That is the last place you want to be.

Summary: How should a Christian acquire knowledge?

When I examine an area I spend six months to a year on the topic.

1. I look up all the verses of Scripture related to the topic.
2. I meditate on these verses (not study but meditate - see Appendix B).

3. I examine my experiences in light of the meditated insights I am receiving, and seek to bring my life's experiences into line with what I am learning.

4. I explore what others before me and around me have learned and experienced in the area.

5. I leave the area when I sense my life is a living demonstration of what is taught in the Scriptures.

6. I believe the Bible is to be experienced in our lives, not just studied.

7. I believe the anointing of the Holy Spirit is what makes this all happen. The Holy Spirit calls me into the area, leads me in the discovery process, and anoints my experiences so I can see, understand and live spiritual truths.

The Pharisees Always Resist the Holy Spirit

I think we all need to beware of any levels of Phariseeism within ourselves. Pharisees do not use the biblical approach for discovering truth. They do not depend on the Holy Spirit in their processes for discovering truth. They ignore the Holy Spirit and live out of biblical law and rational theology, rather than out of the Word and the Spirit as Jesus did (Jn. 5:19,20,30).

You will recall that the Pharisees always stoned the prophets, and even killed Jesus (Acts 7:52). Not that the Pharisees didn't love God. They did. They thought they were doing God a favor by killing Jesus. And they loved the Word of God. However, they loved their traditions too much. They used their traditions to invalidate portions of the Word of God and to explain why they no longer needed to be kept (Matt. 15:3-9). Each of us must examine our lives diligently to be sure we have not fallen into the trap of becoming a modern-day Pharisee (II Cor. 13:5).

The Bible is **crystal clear** that the Christian is to live and walk in the Spirit (Gal. 5:25), to pray in the Spirit (Jude 20), to be filled with the Spirit (Eph. 5:18), and to worship in spirit (Jn. 4:23). The Spirit is that inner, energizing force, not matter from the outside. He is a Person Whose Presence is felt as a spiritual energy which is sometimes referred to as "the anointing."

To reduce life to matter alone is to remove the power of the Holy Spirit from the experiences of life and to focus on the worship of the false gods of our culture - rationalism, humanism, and a mechanistic approach to the universe rather than a vital one. The Bible (Col. 1:17) and the most up-to-date science ($E = MC^2$) both confirm that energy is at the core of the universe. The energy of God holds this universe together (Col. 1:17).

The Fearful Pull Back

Fear is a motivating force satan uses effectively in many people. The Bible makes it abundantly clear that perfect love casts out fear (I Jn. 4:18).

The Spirit-filled Christian will be moved by faith joined with the aggressive commission of Jesus Christ to disciple all nations (Matt. 28:19).

The fearful are afraid of everything new, of every challenge, and of forces around them that they can't control or understand. In their fear, they generally come against all new ideas, cower at every new challenge, and hide from the powerful forces they assume to be hostile.

The PHARISEES AND THE FEARFUL resist what the Spirit of God is doing in the world in their day.

Beware that you not become trapped in their snares. You will recognize them by their unwillingness to incorporate the working of the Holy Spirit in their lives or their methodology for discovering truth. They move in fear, resisting what God is doing in the earth in their day. They carry with them the spirit of murder, and always stone the messenger who brings word of the new thing God is doing in their midst (Acts 7:51,52).

To safeguard, use a biblical approach for discovering truth and move in spiritual knowledge and faith. I recommend listening only to teachers who do the same. Learn to hear the voice of God, so you can be filled with the Lord's words of hope and comfort. Jesus said, "My sheep hear My voice" (Jn. 10:27).

Only those who seek truth find truth!

Blessed are they which do hunger and thirst after righteousness: for they shall be filled (Matt. 5:6).

Blessed are the pure in heart: for they shall see God (Matt. 5:8).

Some people do not hunger and thirst after righteousness. (Righteousness, of course, embodies truth.) Some hunger and thirst to prove themselves right. Some people do not have a pure heart. Instead they hunger and thirst to prove others wrong.

Attitude is everything!

For example, one gentleman, who was in charge of producing a major "medical" bulletin for a well-known and well-respected evangelical Bible teacher, evaluated modern alternative medical approaches. He offered this comment: "I started out to prove that these alternative methods were quackery, and I found out that they were occult."

Well, when you start out with the objective of proving someone is a quack, you have begun your search with impure motives and your search for truth is defiled and will not be fulfilled. You have taken an adversarial attitude in your heart. This is strictly forbidden in Scriptures. It is satan who is the adversary and accuser (Matt. 13:39; Rev. 12:10,11). We are not to take on his heart when we search for truth. We are to take on the heart of the Holy Spirit. We are to come alongside and comfort (Jn. 14:16,17).

When the Bereans heard a NEW teaching, they did not try to prove it wrong; they tried to prove it right (Acts 17:11). Let us be more noble-minded, as the Bereans were, and seek to prove people RIGHT, not prove them wrong. Of course, in the above illustration, the "Bible teacher" was able to prove that ALL alternative approaches to medicine were false, and that the allopathic approach to medicine used by traditional doctors today and which focuses on the use of drugs was "biblical." What other outcome would be possible, given his starting point?

Hopefully these few thoughts will help you in thinking through a Spirit-led, biblical approach for processing new ideas.

APPENDIX A

HOW TO BE BORN AGAIN

Jesus said, "Except a man be born again, he cannot see the kingdom of God" (Jn. 3:3). What does it mean to be born again? Why would I need to be born again? What do I need to do to become born again?

Man was created hollow at his core. We are vessels needing to be filled (II Cor. 4:7); we are temples needing to be inhabited by (a) God (I Cor. 6:19). The God of this universe, Yahweh, desires to fill and direct you from within. He desires to commune with you and to have fellowship with you from within your heart and spirit.

This He will do if you invite Him into your life, your heart and your soul. He enters when you give over the reins of your life to Him, when you acknowledge His rightful position as your Lord and Savior. Then He takes His place upon the throne of your life, washes away your sin, and restores fellowship with you through His Holy Spirit. He actually joins Himself to you and begins to flow effortlessly out from deep within your heart (I Cor. 6:17).

So, you need to ask yourself, "Who rules my life? Have I given it over to the Lord, the Creator of the universe, or do I rule it?" (Is. 53:6). If you have not given the control of your life to the Lord Jesus Christ, then you need to do so now in a prayer of repentance. Pray the following from your heart.

"Dear Lord God, I acknowledge You as my Lord and my Savior. I repent and turn from going my own sinful way, and I acknowledge that You have the right to the reins of my life. I place my life back under Your control where it should have been from day one.

"I acknowledge my sinfulness and self-will and stubbornness, and I turn from these sins and from the many other sins which come from my independent living. I acknowledge You as the One to Whom I will come for direction for my life from now on. I ask that the blood of Your Son Jesus Christ, which was shed on Calvary, be applied to my sins and wash them away as far as the east is from the west. Let them be remembered no more.

"Teach me Your ways. Instruct me in the way that I should go. From this day on, I look to You as my Lord and my Savior. Thank You for Your gift of eternal life, of life both now and in eternity. I worship You, Lord. In Jesus' Name, Amen."

This prayer, prayed from your heart, makes you a child of God and grants you eternal life in heaven with Him. It also re-connects you to the river of God within your being, so that your life here on earth will become much more full and rewarding. Welcome into the Kingdom of God.

If you have prayed this prayer for the very first time, we encourage you to seek out a local church embracing both the Bible and the Spirit so that you may grow together with other believers.

APPENDIX B

BIBLICAL MEDITATION

An example of revelation knowledge is while reading the Bible a verse leaps off the page, hits you between the eyes and God says, "This is for you right now." These are precious experiences for the believer. However, for many, they do not happen often enough. There are seven things I do that grant me the privilege of receiving revelation knowledge every time I read the Bible. Truth and insights leap off the page and an understanding of how they are to adjust my life permeates my spirit and soul. I love this experience and hunger for it every time I read the Scriptures. That is why I prepare myself by doing the following seven things. Prayerfully reflect on these steps and determine which ones you do and don't use.

Biblical Meditation
Resulting in illumination, revelation knowledge, anointed reasoning

Do Not Do This:	But Do This:
Left-brain Study/Rational Humanism	Whole-brain/Heart Meditation/Divine Revelation
1. Have unconfessed sin	1. Be washed by Jesus' blood
2. Have a pre-conceived attitude	2. Have a teachable attitude
3. Be independent: "I can..."	3. Pray: "Lord, show me"
4. Read quickly	4. Slow down, ponder, muse
5. Rely on reason & analysis only	5. Combine anointed reason, flowing pictures, music & speech
6. Read without specific purpose	6. Read with focused purpose
7. Take credit for insights	7. Glorify God for insights

The Seven Steps of Biblical Meditation explained:

1. **Lord, cleanse me by Your blood:** Since receiving divine revelation is at the heart of biblical meditation, you must prepare yourself to receive from the Holy Spirit by repenting and being cleansed by the blood of the Lamb. You must be obedient to previous revelations from God (Matt. 7:6), and confess any sin in your life, so you are not cut off from ongoing revelation (Is. 59:1,2; I Jn. 1:9).

2. **Lord, grant me a teachable attitude:** Revelation is given to those who maintain an attitude of humility, and it is withheld from the proud and the arrogant. So keep an open, humble attitude before God, allowing Him the freedom to shed greater light on any ideas you currently hold and to alter them as He sees fit (Jas. 4:6; II Pet. 1:19).

3. **Lord, I will not use my faculties myself:** You can do nothing of your own initiative but only what you hear and see by the Spirit (Jn. 5:19,20,30). You do not have a mind to use, but a mind to present to God so He can use it and fill it with anointed reason and divine vision (Prov. 3:5-7; Rom. 12:1,2). If you use your mind yourself, it is a dead work (Heb. 6:1,2).

4. **Lord, I pray that the eyes of my heart might be enlightened:** Slow down as you read, mulling the text over and over in your heart and mind, praying constantly for God to give you a spirit of wisdom and revelation in the knowledge of Him (Eph. 1:17,18; Ps. 119:18).

5. **Lord, I present the abilities to reason and to imagine to You to fill and flow through by Your Spirit:** Meditation involves presenting your faculties to God for Him to fill and use. These include your left-brain reasoning abilities as well as your right-brain visual capacities. Look for the river of God (i.e. "Spirit flow") to guide and fill both hemispheres, granting you anointed reasoning and dream and vision (Jn. 7:37-39). Music can assist you, as can muttering, speaking, and writing as you go through the discovery process (II Kings 3:15).

6. **Lord, show me the solution to the problem I am facing:** Focused attention brings additional energies of concentration of heart and mind, which help release revelation. For example, note the difference between a ray of sunlight hitting a piece of paper, and sunlight going through a magnifying glass to hit a piece of paper. The focused energy creates a ray so concentrated that the paper bursts into flames. When you have a hunger to master a new understanding and discipline, that hungry and searching heart will cause you to see things you would not normally see (Matt. 5:6).

7. **Thank You, Lord, for what You have shown me:** Realizing that the revelation came from the indwelling Holy Spirit, give all the glory to God for what has been revealed (Eph. 3:21).

Another Great Aid to "Seeing": Writing Out Scripture

When you write or type out a verse, you discover words which you otherwise might have missed. Therefore, I write out verses which I know are key truths for my life. I pray over them, diagram them, analyze them, and meditate upon them. That is why I have written many of my books. I write so I can learn, so I can put truths I understand in my own words and in a framework, which is meaningful for me.

The following is the law God gave for new kings who had just been crowned and were coming to sit upon their throne for the first time:

> *"Now it shall come about when he sits on the throne of his kingdom, he shall write for himself a copy of this law on a scroll in the presence of the Levitical priests" (Deut. 17:18).*

Since we are kings and priests, are we to do any less (I Pet 2:9)? Let us make the writing out of Scriptures an important part of our lives.

APPENDIX C

FOUR KEYS TO HEARING GOD'S VOICE

The age in which we live is so married to rationalism and cognitive, analytical thought that we almost mock when we hear of one actually claiming to be able to hear the voice of God. However, we do not scoff, for several reasons. First, men and women throughout the Bible heard God's voice. Also, there are some highly effective and reputable men and women of God alive today who demonstrate that they hear God's voice. Finally, there is a deep hunger within us all to commune with God, and hear Him speak within our hearts.

As a born-again, Bible-believing Christian, I struggled unsuccessfully for years to hear God's voice. I prayed, fasted, studied my Bible and listened for a voice within, all to no avail. There was no inner voice that I could hear! Then God set me aside for a year to study, read, and experiment in the area of learning to hear His voice. During that time, the Lord taught me four keys that opened the door to two-way prayer. I have discovered that not only do they work for me, but they have worked for many thousands of believers who have been taught to use them, bringing tremendous intimacy to their Christian experience and transforming their very way of living. This will happen to you also as you seek God, utilizing the following four keys. They are all found in Habakkuk 2:1,2. I encourage you to read this passage before going on.

Key #1 - God's voice in our hearts sounds like a flow of spontaneous thoughts. Therefore, when I tune to God, I tune to spontaneity.

The Bible says that the Lord answered me and said...(Hab. 2:2). Habakkuk knew the sound of God's voice. Elijah described it as a still, small voice (I Kings 19:12). I had always listened for an inner audible voice, and surely God can and does speak that way at times. However, I have found that for most of us, most of the time, **God's inner voice comes to us as spontaneous thoughts, visions, feelings, or impressions.** For example, hasn't each of us had the experience of driving down the road and having a thought come to us to pray for a certain person? We generally acknowledge this to be the voice of God calling us to pray for that individual. My question to you is "What did God's voice sound like as you drove in your car? Was it an inner, audible voice, or was it a spontaneous thought that lit upon your mind?" Most of you would say that God's voice came to you as a spontaneous thought.

So I thought to myself, "Maybe when I listen for God's voice, I should be listening for a flow of spontaneous thoughts. Maybe spirit-level communication is received as spontaneous thoughts, impressions, feelings, and visions." Through experimentation and feedback from thousands of others, I am now convinced that this is so.

The Bible confirms this in many ways. The definition of paga, the Hebrew word for intercession, is "a chance encounter or an accidental intersecting." When God lays people on our hearts for intercession, He does it through paga, a chance-encounter thought, accidentally intersecting our thought processes. Therefore, when I tune to God, I tune to chance-encounter thoughts or spontaneous thoughts. When I am poised quietly before God in prayer, I have found that the flow of spontaneous thoughts that comes is quite definitely from God.

Key #2 - I must learn to still my own thoughts and emotions, so that I can sense God's flow of thoughts and emotions within me.

Habakkuk said, "I will stand on my guard post and station myself on the rampart..." (Hab. 2:1). Habakkuk knew that in order to hear God's quiet, inner, spontaneous thoughts, he had to first go to a quiet place and still his own thoughts and emotions. Psalm 46:10 encourages us to be still, and know that He is God. There is a deep inner knowing (spontaneous flow) in our spirits that each of us can experience when we quiet our flesh and our minds.

I have found several simple ways to quiet myself so that I can more readily pick up God's spontaneous flow. Loving God through a quiet worship song is a most effective means for me (note II Kings 3:15). It is as I become still (thoughts, will, and emotions) and am poised before God that the divine flow is realized. Therefore, after I worship quietly and then become still, I open myself for that spontaneous flow. If thoughts come to me of things I have forgotten to do, I write them down and then dismiss them. If thoughts of guilt or unworthiness come to my mind, I repent thoroughly, receive the washing of the blood of the Lamb, and put on His robe of righteousness, seeing myself spotless before the presence of God (Is. 61:10; Col. 1:22).

As I fix my gaze upon Jesus (Heb. 12:2), becoming quiet in His presence, and sharing with Him what is on my heart, I find that two-way dialogue begins to flow. Spontaneous thoughts flow from the throne of God to me, and I find that I am actually conversing with the King of Kings.

It is very important that you become still and properly focused if you are going to receive the pure word of God. If you are not still, you will simply be receiving your own thoughts. If you are not properly focused on Jesus, you will receive an impure flow, because the intuitive flow comes out of that upon which you have fixed your eyes. Therefore, if you fix your eyes upon Jesus, the intuitive flow comes from Jesus. If you fix your gaze upon some desire of your heart, the intuitive flow comes out of that desire of your heart. To have a pure flow you must first of all become still, and secondly, you must carefully fix your eyes upon Jesus. Again, quietly worshiping the King, and then receiving out of the stillness that follows quite easily accomplish this.

Key #3 - As I pray, I fix the eyes of my heart upon Jesus, seeing in the spirit the dreams and visions of Almighty God.

We have already alluded to this principle in the previous paragraphs; however, we need to develop it a bit further. Habakkuk said, "I will keep watch to see," and God said, "Record the vision" (Hab. 2:1,2). It is very interesting that Habakkuk was going to actually start looking for vision as he prayed. He was going to open the eyes of his heart, and look into the spirit world to see what God wanted to show him. This is an intriguing idea.

I had never thought of opening the eyes of my heart and looking for vision. However, the more I thought of it, the more I realized this was exactly what God intends for me to do. He gave me eyes in my heart. They are to be used to see in the spirit world the vision and movement of Almighty God. I believe there is an active spirit world functioning all around me. This world is full of angels, demons, the Holy Spirit, the omnipresent God, and His omnipresent Son, Jesus. There is no reason for me not to see it, other than my rational culture, which tells me not to believe it is even there and provides no instruction on how to become open to seeing this spirit world.

The most obvious prerequisite to seeing is that we need to look. Daniel was seeing a vision in his mind and he said, "I was looking...I kept looking...I kept looking" (Dan. 7:2,9,13). Now as I pray, I look for Jesus present with me, and I watch Him as He speaks to me, doing and saying the things that are on His heart. Many Christians will find that if they will only look, they will see. Jesus is Emmanuel, God with us (Matt. 1:23). It is as simple as that. You will see a spontaneous inner vision in a manner similar to receiving spontaneous inner thoughts. You can see Christ present with you in a comfortable setting, because **Christ *is present with you in a comfortable setting. Actually, you will probably discover that inner vision comes so easily you will have a tendency to reject it, thinking that it is just you. (Doubt*** *is satan's most effective weapon against the Church.) However, if you will persist in recording these visions, your doubt will soon be overcome by faith as you recognize that the content of them could only be birthed in Almighty God.*

God continually revealed Himself to His covenant people using dream and vision. He did so from Genesis to Revelation and said that, since the Holy Spirit was poured out in Acts 2, we should expect to receive a continuing flow of dreams and visions (Acts 2:1-4,17). Jesus, our perfect Example, demonstrated this ability of living out of ongoing contact with Almighty God. He said that He did nothing on His own initiative, but only that which He *saw the Father doing, and heard the Father saying (Jn. 5:19,20,30). What an incredible way to live!*

Is it actually possible for us to live out of the divine initiative as Jesus did? A major purpose of Jesus' death and resurrection was that the veil be torn from top to bottom, giving us access into the immediate presence of God, and we are commanded to draw near (Lk. 23:45; Heb. 10: 19-22). Therefore, even though what I am describing seems a bit unusual to a rational twentieth-century culture, it is demonstrated and described as being a central biblical teaching and experience. It is time to restore to the Church all that belongs to the Church.

Because of their intensely rational nature and existence in an overly rational culture, some will need more assistance and understanding of these truths before they can move into them. They will find this help in the book Communion With God by the same authors.

Key #4 - Journaling, the writing out of our prayers and God's answers, provides a great new freedom in hearing God's voice.

God told Habakkuk to record the vision and inscribe it on tablets...(Hab. 2:2). It had never crossed my mind to write out my prayers and God's answers as Habakkuk did at God's command. If you begin to search Scripture for this idea, you will find hundreds of chapters demonstrating it (Psalms, many of the prophets, Revelation). Why then hadn't I ever thought of it?

I called the process "journaling," and I began experimenting with it. I discovered it to be a fabulous facilitator to clearly discerning God's inner; spontaneous flow because as I journaled I was able to write **in faith for long periods of time,** simply believing it was God. I did not have to test it as I was receiving it (which jams one's receiver), because I knew that when the flow was over I **could go back and test and examine it carefully,** making sure that it lined up with Scripture.

You will be amazed when you attempt journaling. Doubt may hinder you at first, but throw it off, reminding yourself that it is a biblical concept, and that God is present, speaking to His children. Don't take yourself too seriously. When you do, you become tense and get in the way of the Holy Spirit's movement. It is when we cease our labors and enter His rest that God is free to flow (Heb. 4:10). Therefore, put a smile on your face, sit back comfortably, get out your pen and paper, and turn your attention toward God in praise and worship, seeking His face. As you write out your question to God and become still, fixing your gaze on Jesus, Who is present with you, you will suddenly have a very good thought in response to your question. Don't doubt. Simply write it down. Later, as you read your journaling, you, too, will be blessed to discover that you are indeed dialoguing with God.

Some final notes. No one should attempt this without having first read through at least the New Testament (preferably, the entire Bible), nor should one attempt this unless he is submitted to solid, spiritual leadership. All major directional moves that come through journaling should be submitted before being acted upon.

You can order the *Communion With God Study Guide* online at www.CWGMinistries.org or call 1-800-466-6961. A complete catalog of over 50 books available by Mark & Patti Virkler as well as 100 college courses through external degree is available at the website. Email: info@cwgministries.org